REASONS TO BELIEVE

Other Books by Scott Hahn

The Lamb's Supper: The Mass as Heaven on Earth

Hail, Holy Queen: The Mother of God in the Word of God

First Comes Love: Finding Your Family in the Church and the Trinity

Lord, Have Mercy: The Healing Power of Confession

Swear to God: The Promise and Power of the Sacraments

Letter and Spirit: From Written Text to Living Word in the Liturgy

Ordinary Work, Extraordinary Grace: My Spiritual Journey in Opus Dei

Understanding the Scriptures: A Complete Course on Bible Study

Scripture Matters: Essays on Reading the Bible from the Heart of the Church

Understanding "Our Father": Biblical Reflections on the Lord's Prayer

A Father Who Keeps His Promises: God's Covenant Love in Scripture

Rome Sweet Rome: Our Journey to Catholicism (with Kimberly Hahn)

Living the Mysteries: A Guide for Unfinished Christians (with Mike Aquilina)

For online Bible studies and resources by Scott Hahn, visit www.salvationhistory.com. For a catalog of over 500 titles of Scott Hahn's talks on tape (or CD), contact Saint Joseph Communications in West Covina, CA (phone: 1-800-526-2151, online: www.saintjoe.com).

REASONS TO BELIEVE

How to Understand, Explain, and Defend
the Catholic Faith

SCOTT HAHN

DOUBLEDAY

New York • London • Toronto • Sydney • Auckland

PUBLISHED BY DOUBLEDAY

Published in the United States by Doubleday, an imprint of The Doubleday Broadway Publishing Group, a division of Random House, Inc., New York. www.doubleday.com

DOUBLEDAY and the portrayal of an anchor with a dolphin are registered trademarks of Random House, Inc.

Book design by Michael Collica
Frontispiece courtesy of Art Resource

Library of Congress Cataloging-in-Publication Data
Hahn, Scott.
Reasons to believe : how to understand, explain, and defend the Catholic faith / by Scott Hahn.
p. cm.
Includes bibliographical references.
ISBN-13: 978-0-385-50935-0 (alk. paper)   1. Catholic Church—Apologetic works.   2. Catholic Church—Doctrines.   I. Title.
BX1752.H23 2007
230'.2—dc22
2007007526

Nihil Obstat: Monsignor Michael F. Hull, STD, Censor Librorum.
Imprimatur: Most Reverend Robert A. Brucato, Auxiliary Bishop and Vicar General, Archdiocese of New York.

The Nihil Obstat and Imprimatur are official declarations that a book or pamphlet is free of doctrinal or moral error. No implication is contained therein that those who have granted the Nihil Obstat and the Imprimatur agree with the content, opinions, or statements expressed.

PRINTED IN THE UNTIED STATES OF AMERICA

1   3   5   7   9   10 8   6   4   2

First Edition

To David Timothy Bonaventure Hahn

On the occasion of his First Communion
and the royal-priestly anointing of Confirmation

Contents

III *Royal Reasons*

Natural Reasons

One

More than a Feeling

On the Love of Learning and the
Desire for Dunking

I was the freshest of freshmen.

Like almost everyone in that incoming class, I was living away
from my home and family for the first time, and I was hungry for
everything that Grove City College had promised us. Indeed, I'm
sure that I wanted it more than most of my classmates. I had been
an academically inclined high school student, the type who was
tempted to capitalize the word "Learning" when it was used as a
noun. I was a relatively new Christian, but already steeped in theology, and there at Grove City College I could study with noted
thinkers of the evangelical and Calvinist worlds.

What's more, Grove City was not an isolated Christian institution. It was part of a cultural movement. Two other evangelical
Calvinist campuses sprawled nearby, Westminster College and
Geneva College, and all the lands in between those campuses and
ours—mostly small towns and farming communities—were dot-
ted with pastoral and communal experiments that drew inspira-
tion, energy, and even members from the colleges.

So, as I took my first steps away from home and into the wider world, I had a true freshman's openness to new experiences and ideas. And the college and its orbit had plenty to occupy my mind and senses. Still, it wasn't an easy transition for me. The college couldn't fit all the first-year men in the freshmen dorms, so some were dispersed to live with the upperclassmen. I was among the dispersed.

The upperclassmen were kind and welcoming; but, I have to admit, I felt isolated. Some of this feeling, I'm sure, was just garden-variety homesickness. Some of it, too, was the sense of being the "odd man out" among a horde of old buddies—the guy to whom they had to explain all their inside jokes. But a big part of it was a mismatch of interests and ideals: here I was, eager for Learning and intellectual companionship—maybe even a disputation or two. And there *they* were, world-weary juniors and seniors, for whom college had long been demystified and its professors demythologized.

Gradually, though, I reached out across the gulf that separated me from my fellow freshmen. I got to know two guys, Doug and Ron, especially well, as they shared my interests and my longing for like-minded—but, even more, like-hearted—Christian fellowship. Those two were easily the most popular first-year men on campus. Getting to know them over the opening weeks of the semester, I heard a lot about the church they attended. In fact, Doug and Ron were so enthusiastic about it, they talked about little else; and all other subjects seemed to lead them back to the main theme of their conversation, which was their newfound church.

"Dunked for Real"

The place was more than ten miles away, between our campus and Westminster's. Every Sunday its worship service was standing-room-only. The singing raised the roof; the preaching was electric.

The congregation was a mix of local farmers and students and professors from the colleges. They had built up a network of social services, including adoption, foster care, and programs for troubled youth. Every service ended with a "laying on of hands," at which people were apparently healed of ailments ranging from depression to cancer. Every month or so, after the service, many new members would be baptized by total immersion in the nearby creek.

These events were the favored topic of conversation on the way to and from classes, and they were the inevitable destination of our table talk in the dining hall. A few weeks into the semester, I finally agreed to join my newfound friends for their Sunday worship.

Our anticipation grew during the long ride out to church. And the service itself didn't disappoint us. There was exuberant singing, powerful preaching, and the laying on of hands. I found myself wondering why my Presbyterian worship couldn't be this way. My church generated excitement in special programs like Young Life, but we could accomplish it only by segregating teens from the staid older folks and the distraction of small children. Yet here was a true cross-section of local life, and it was alive and engaged.

On the drive back to campus, Doug and Ron began talking about how soon they might make their own trip to the creek for baptism. There was no question *whether* this would be the next step. The only question was *when*.

And it was only then—when they began speaking in terms of baptism—that my own mind stopped racing with excitement. Indeed, the racing vehicle screeched to halt. The conversation continued back on campus, where a number of students were talking about getting "dunked for real."

We had all been baptized as infants, but now my friends were repudiating the very idea of infant baptism. When I raised a caution, they replied, "Scott, what do you remember from your baptism?" On the other hand, they pointed out, we all could vividly remember what we had seen, heard, and felt at our newfound country church that very day—a church whose truth was evidenced in apparent miracles.

I still hesitated. "But is it biblical to get baptized again? And are you sure that infant baptism is unbiblical?"

One of the guys answered my question with a question: "Okay, Scott, where do you see infant baptism in the New Testament?"

I had no ready answer.

Rebaptism and Research

My friends weren't ridiculing me. They were merely discouraging what they saw as my "overly intellectual hang-ups." Don't get me wrong: they were very intelligent kids. They just felt they didn't need further reasons after the continued experience of such exalted worship. They felt that their experience was reason enough for them to take action.

The problem occupied my mind. These new friends meant a lot to me, and their church excited me. But the prospect of rebaptism troubled me, and I wasn't sure why. I decided to mention it to a professor I deeply respected, Dr. Robert VandeKappelle. I was taking his course titled Biblical Ideas, and I was loving it. The ink wasn't yet dry on Dr. VandeKappelle's doctorate from Princeton, and his love for scholarship shone in his lectures and in his smiling eyes. With his wire-rimmed glasses and conservative neckties, he even looked the part of the prof. Gently inquisitive, he fostered the kind of Learning I'd dreamt about when I first applied to Grove City College.

In his office one afternoon, I mentioned, as casually as I could, that some friends and I were planning to get rebaptized.

He raised an eyebrow above the wire rims, but his eyes kept smiling, and he spoke gently as always. "Rebaptized? Why?"

He knew, of course, about the church we were attending. Everybody knew about it.

I said, "I was baptized as a baby, and it didn't mean anything to me."

He kept smiling. "So?"

"Besides," I said, "where is it in the New Testament?"

Still smiling, he asked, "Have you looked into it?"

My silence answered him well enough. He said, "Well, maybe you should," and then the clincher: "Scott, why not make infant baptism the topic for your research paper in my class?"

The next Sunday my friends got "dunked," but I stayed back and worshiped closer to campus. Meanwhile, I had checked out all the books the college library had to offer on the subject of infant baptism, a contentious issue from the earliest days of the Protestant Reformation, dividing the classic Reformed strains (Lutheran and Calvinist) from the Anabaptist (Baptist and Mennonite). I loaded the volumes onto my library card, into my backpack, and into my dorm room, where I pored over them late into the night.

What did I learn? I learned that the custom of infant baptism was very ancient indeed, and those who held on to it had good scriptural reasons for doing so. Jesus Himself had said: "Let the children come to me, and do not hinder them; for to such *belongs* the kingdom of heaven" (Mt 19:14). The Lord made clear that the *kingdom* belongs to those *children*, and baptism is somehow the sign of the kingdom's coming (see Mt 28:18–19). When Peter preached the Gospel for the first time on the first Pentecost, he put the matter in the same terms: "Repent, and be baptized every one of you in the name of Jesus Christ for the forgiveness of your sins; and you shall receive the gift of the Holy Spirit. For the promise is to you *and to your children*" (Acts 2:38–39).

These New Testament passages made the case for infant baptism plausible to me, if not quite as explicit as I would have preferred. But when I read the reasons that scholars and sages had marshaled from the *whole* Bible—*both* testaments—the case was overwhelming. When I considered Jesus' "New Covenant" in light of the history of God's covenants with His people, I saw that provision was always made for the inclusion of infants. If God welcomed newborns into Israel by means of ritual circumcision for two thousand years, why would He suddenly close the kingdom to babies because they could not understand ritual baptism? And if He had intended to make such a radical change in the terms of the covenant, wouldn't He have said so explicitly?

When I read the New Testament in light of the Old, the New became more luminously clear. And I knew what course I should take—and what course I should not take—in my life as a Christian. I had reasons to believe what my Calvinist ancestors and teachers had believed about infant baptism.

I will not bore you with a detailed summary of the paper I wrote. Suffice it to say that I made a firm decision not to be rebaptized. And I did get an A from Dr. VandeKappelle. Then I joined one of those staid and lackluster local congregations—a congregation that baptized infants "for real" and that worshiped in more conventional ways.

College had given me my first experience of disciplined Learning as well as a life-changing Learning experience. I learned to test every spirit—to check my feelings against right reason, and to check my reasoned hunches against the Christian churches' heritage of reflection on biblical faith. It is this method that would, some years later, give me reasons to believe in the claims of the Roman Catholic Church, and then to be received into full communion with that Church. But that's another story, for another book.

BE PREPARED

The moral of the story in *this* book was set forth many years ago, in the First Letter of St. Peter: "Always be prepared to make a defense to any one who calls you to account for the hope that is in you, yet do it with gentleness and reverence" (1 Pet 3:15).

There are times in life when we have to make a leap into darkness, go with our gut instinct, or settle for blind faith. But those are not "normal" times. They're usually times of extreme emergency. We shouldn't strive to live our lives in a constant state of crisis. Our ordinary way is evident from St. Peter's use of the word "always." We should, like the Boy Scouts, always "be prepared" to explain the reasons why we believe what we believe. That statement assumes that our beliefs are defensible on rational grounds, and that we're willing to spend a lifetime preparing to defend what we profess in the articles of faith. When I was an undergraduate, I was vulnerable because I had never bothered to study the meaning of baptism. Yet I was intensely aware of how I *felt* when I was in that zealous, rebaptizing congregation. What I needed to learn was that the laws of God, like the law of gravity, do not depend upon how I *feel* about them. They are inexorable, and God has willed them to be knowable, even in the absence of strong emotion or apparent miracles.

I needed to learn how to place my reason at the service of the mystery of baptism. For baptism is a sacred sign instituted by Jesus Christ, but made up of the most common and unimposing matter: water.

After thirty-one more years of Christian living, I'm still learning that lesson, and I hope to be learning it on the day I die, because the mysteries of Christianity are unfathomable. They're a participation in the very life of God, and none of us will ever be able to attain mastery over God's life. Again, the mysteries are unfathomable—inexhaustible—but they are eminently knowable, because *God Himself has willed them to be known.* That is the very reason He revealed Himself in the book of Scripture. That is the very reason for His self-disclosure in creation, "the book of nature."

God and His ways are understandable and defensible; and, as Christians, we have the sweet obligation of coming to know them and coming to their defense as often as we please. There is no shortage of opportunity for study, contemplation, and evangelization. Wherever we go, we are in God's presence and in His world. And in most places we go we can take a good book along for stolen moments of study. It's the work of a lifetime.

SEEDS OF THE WORD

This book is a summons for Catholics to fulfill the duty that St. Peter spelled out. It's not enough for us just to *feel* hopeful, and then hope that our hope will be contagious. St. Peter wants us to prepare a defensible account of our hope, showing that its foundations are unshakable, grounded as they are in ultimate reality.

Again, we're talking about much more than a feeling. We're talking about theology. Specifically, we're talking about that branch of theology known as apologetics—the art of explaining and defending the faith. Students of history perhaps know that there is, among the ancient Church Fathers, a category called "the apologists." These were men who took it upon themselves to spell out Christian doctrine in terms that ordinary non-Christians might understand.

They appealed not so much to God's special revelation—not to the Bible or the creeds—but to logic, science, nature, history, and common sense. They even appealed to the highest principles of pagan philosophy and religion, showing that these were better fulfilled by Christianity! One of the Church's greatest early defenders, St. Justin Martyr, distilled this approach to a handy principle: "whatever is true is ours." Since God created the world and everything in it—including the pagan philosophers—Justin could treat almost everything he encountered as "seeds of the Word."

This was true of many of the apologists. Not all of them were as polite and "catholic" in their tastes as Justin was, but most of them took special care to provide reasoned responses to their contemporaries' objections to Christian doctrine and practice—even when those objections were slanderous, untrue, or downright surreal.

Well, like those ancient Fathers, we live in a culture that is baffled by Christianity and skeptical of the Church's claims to divine revelation. We live in a culture that often caricatures faith as being nothing more than credulity, bigotry, and superstition. And there is no shortage of people who want us to step up and give a credible accounting for the things we believe. Some of them are hostile; some are curious; some are amused; and some are sincerely searching. In any case, and in every case, we, like our ancient ancestors, need to take up the art of apologetics. We must be ready to give our reasoned defense.

Step one is simple. We mustn't be "ashamed of the Gospel" (Rom 1:16). We mustn't be ashamed of the things that unbelievers despise and disdain. We mustn't be afraid to take ownership of the gifts God had given us—gifts like Christian dogma. The historian Lionel Trilling, an agnostic, observed that "when the dogmatic principle in religion is slighted, religion goes along for a while on generalized emotion and ethical intention—'morality touched by emotion,' " but soon it "loses the force of its impulse and even the essence of its being."

For secularists, dogma is the antithesis of reason. It is—or so they believe—something imposed upon the mind from outside, and imposed with violence, against the very nature of the mind. It's the job of the Christian apologist to demonstrate that the dogmas of faith are compatible with reason. Though the articles of the creed often surpass the limits of human reasoning power, they are not unreasonable.

But secularists are not the only ones who take a dim view of dogma. For my college buddies and me—though we were devout Christians—dogma had almost become irrelevant when compared to the intensity of our feelings at those worship services. We feared that the sober study of dogma might threaten our faith, dampen our zeal, or even mock the marvels of God.

We were wrong, as Dr. VandeKappelle allowed me to discover. We Christians must "always be prepared to make a defense."

ROTE TO REASON

Yet, as the old saying goes: the best defense is a good offense. Apologetics should never be merely a grown-up and Christian version of *Mad* magazine's *Snappy Answers to Stupid Questions* (a book I devoured when I was a kid). We're not looking for the quick comeback that will silence our obnoxious neighbors or coworkers. We're looking for answers that will satisfy—first ourselves and then others. Apologetics is a theological art that must rest on a firm foundation of theological science. If our defense does not flow from deep preparation, deep Christian formation, it will be unconvincing at best, but merely offensive at worst.

"Snappy answers" are not what St. Peter wanted, and they're not what God wants. He wants us to have well-trained Christian minds—minds formed by profound study, by penance, and by prayer—minds that are formed *for* humility and generosity. The answers that arise from such minds hold far more persuasive power than those that spring merely from memory (though memorization, too, has its place).

As Catholics, we need to stretch ourselves. We should first desire to make a serious study of doctrine and Scripture, history and philosophy. If we don't feel that desire, we should pray for God to give it to us as a gift, a grace. Then we should apply ourselves to the task anyway, even if we don't feel like it, and especially if we find the subject difficult. The rewards are richer, the more trying the task. Just ask the patriarch Jacob, who labored fourteen years in order to win his beloved Rachel in marriage (Gen 29).

Nevertheless, I want to make this study as painless as possible for you. This book will begin by sketching out some basics of reasoned faith—giving "reasons to believe" for those who raise common objections against theism and Catholicism. But such objections usually address just a fragment of the faith, and we want to lead ourselves and others to a faith that is fully integrated. And so we'll proceed, in the final section, to sketch an approach to biblical theology—a faith that is not only reasonable, but also beautiful and full of warmth. If I do my job well, you'll walk away with some new ways of pondering and discussing the faith, but also with a fresh and compelling paradigm for understanding nature (creation), scripture (revelation), and life itself.

In the end, this book is about acquiring a Catholic worldview, a clear-eyed approach to all questions and objections. Back in the 1940s, the monk Eugene Boylan decried the Catholic laity's aversion to the study of dogma: "Where theology is read by the laity, it is usually rather from the point of view of apologetic argument than from that of a dogmatic foundation for true devotion. We would rather see the reverse." A couple of generations later, we should still rather see the reverse. Apologetics will flow most clearly and effectively from a wellspring of dogma and devotion.

The field of Catholic apologetics has yielded an abundant harvest in the last generation. I will not try to duplicate the efforts of authors whose apologetic skills far exceed my own. I stand in awe of their achievements, and I urge you to get to know their work: James Akin, Dave Armstrong, Mark Brumley, Jeff Cavins, David Currie, Father George Duggan, Marcus Grodi, Father John Hardon, S.J., Thomas Howard, Kenneth J. Howell, Karl Keating, Peter Kreeft, Patrick Madrid, Rosalind Moss, Father William Most, Father Mitch Pacina, S.J., Stephen Ray, Alan Schreck, David Scott, Mark Shea, and Tim Staples. They are worthy successors to the ancient apologists, and I invoke their names with admiration, but also with the affection of long-standing friendship. Some of them have been around long enough to have influenced my conversion to Catholicism back in 1986.

When you read the works of these authors, you see the sort of apologetics St. Peter was talking about—apologetics that draws its strength from theology, that is dependent on theology, and that inspires us to pursue theology with a ravenous desire. That's what their work has done for me, and that's why I'm writing this work for you.

Two

OURS TO REASON WHY

On Seeing, Believing, and Flying

I have a friend who was raised in a Christian home, but fell away
from faith for most of his adult life. He wasn't hostile toward religion; he just felt that he and his family didn't need it, so he didn't
really discuss it with his children. The kids grew up aware only
of the stereotypes of religion that recur in movies and on tele-
vision. Now returned to the fold, my friend recently said that his
children, now adults themselves, "pretty much think that religious
people are ignorant. They equate religion with prejudice, back-
wardness, and resistance to progress. Faith, for them, is the opposite of science."

Those presuppositions lie behind many ongoing stories told in
the media. Whether the subject at hand is abortion law, the teaching of evolution, or the debate over Internet pornography, the narrative portrays an era of scientific enlightenment and freedom
besieged by religious forces of superstition and oppression. The
stakes are high, the newspapers warn us. Science's era of triumph
could, at any moment, collapse into a faith-based dark age.

In this story line—the so-called "metanarrative" shared by modernists and postmodernists—Christians are knee-jerk anti-intellectuals whose faith is incompatible with rational thought. The inner life of these imaginary believers would fit Tennyson's description of the minds of brigadiers in battle: "Ours is not to reason why . . . Ours is but to do and die."

Some secularist commentators see faith as being so incompatible with reason that they treat Christianity as a pathological break with reality. I've heard some call it "Christ-psychosis." Those who want to gain a public hearing tend to use milder language. Richard Dawkins and Daniel Dennett, both scientists who are antireligion, take a more positive approach to the problem, describing atheists as "brights" and leaving their hearers to draw the implicit corollary about the dim-witted people who believe in God.

All this will appear strange to believers, who know firsthand that faith is compatible with freedom—in fact, faith is liberating—and who know that faith is compatible with reason—in fact, the groundbreakers in many sciences were devout believers. Witness the accomplishments of Nicolaus Copernicus (a priest) in astronomy, Blaise Pascal (a lay apologist) in mathematics, Gregor Mendel (a monk) in genetics, Louis Pasteur in biology, Antoine Lavoisier in chemistry, John von Neumann in computer science, and Enrico Fermi and Erwin Schrodinger in physics. That's a short list, and it includes only Roman Catholics; a long list could continue for pages. A roster that included other believers—Protestants, Jews, and unconventional theists like Albert Einstein, Fred Hoyle, and Paul Davies—could fill a book.

SOAR ALL OVER

In the real world, in the everyday lives of billions of believers—not least of them scientists—faith and reason coexist without contradiction. I would venture to say that Pope John Paul II was a more precise observer of empirical reality than Drs. Dawkins and Dennett. In beginning his encyclical letter on faith and reason (aptly titled *Faith and Reason*), he put the matter poetically: "Faith and reason are like two wings on which the human spirit rises to the contemplation of truth."

Faith and reason are indeed complementary faculties that we use to think about the truth. When any winged creature (or mechanism) tries to fly on just one wing, it falls to the ground. In a similar way, when we human beings try to wing it with just one faculty, we crash.

I am not saying that non-Christians are unreasonable or unscientific people. I do not wish to dismiss the radical secularists as they have dismissed religious believers. I am saying, however, that all human thinking involves elements of both faith and reason. St. Augustine asserted a fact, not an article of faith, when he stated, "I believe that I may understand." Reason must always proceed from a set of unprovable first principles. This faith is, for the most part, tacit, unacknowledged, or taken for granted; but it is *faith* nonetheless.

We need not consult with Christian saints in order to reach that conclusion. I myself found it first in the work of the twentieth-century scientist Michael Polanyi. A distinguished physical chemist and philosopher, Polanyi effectively demolished the myth of scientific "objectivity" and "detachment." He pointed out that it was impossible for scientific observers to detach themselves from the human condition or from their own culture. He observed that nearly all scientific knowledge proceeded from tacit assumptions and relied upon *trust* in a community of colleagues, in regulations, and in some authority.

A scientist must put *faith* in the experimental data reported by other scientists, and in the institutions that sponsored those scientists, and in the standards by which those scientists received their credentials. A scientist must put faith in the authority of the journals that publish the results of various studies. Finally, but perhaps most fundamentally, a scientist must trust that empirical reality is indeed perceptible and measurable, and that the laws of cause and effect will apply universally. No scientific endeavor can proceed if the experimenter subjects every phenomenon to radical doubt, disqualifying his own observations as well as those of his peers.

Polanyi concluded that science proceeds from a trust that is "fiduciary"—a word that derives from the Latin root meaning "faith-based." Such faith is well placed and well founded, and it enables science to proceed apace; but, nonetheless, it is a species of *faith*, not an absolutely certain knowledge. "We must now recognize belief once more as the source of all knowledge, . . ." Polanyi said. "No intelligence, however critical or original, can operate outside such a fiduciary framework."

Secularism's attempts to replace the authority of religion with a supposed "authority of experience and reason" has proven, in Polanyi's words, "farcically inadequate" and has "enlisted man's highest aspirations in the service of soul-destroying tyrannies."

The alternative to such tyrannies is the realism described by Pope John Paul and by St. Augustine. "Faith and reason are like two wings on which the human spirit rises to the contemplation of truth." "I believe that I may understand."

You don't need to be Christian to affirm those truths—or the other natural conditions of human inquiry. And we should establish these conditions at the outset, because they will provide the common language for our conversation with nonbelievers. For if our hearers disdain the Bible, it will do us no good to cite scriptural proof-texts at them. But logic is quite another matter; and that's where we'll, logically, proceed from here.

FOUR GIVENS

It's a dangerous thing to say that logic is universally recognized, because, in a sense, it's not. There are people today—very intelligent people—who deny the validity of logic. They claim that its laws are merely a manifestation of certain power structures. They argue that logic's force is imaginary, culturally conditioned, Western in origin, or even gender-biased. And all the people who condemn logic in this way do so in ingenious arguments that proceed . . . according to the rules of logic!

It's inescapable. Logic is simply a reflection of how the mind structures its thought, which is itself a reflection of the very structure of reality. The laws of logic may have been articulated by a certain Western philosopher in the ancient world, but they were observed tacitly by his Eastern contemporaries and predecessors.

Logic is an instrument of reason. It is not, as some would have us believe, merely a set of rules for self-consistency. As the inimitable G. K. Chesterton noted, no one is more self-consistent than a madman. If he begins with the fantasy that he is Napoleon, then he rightly draws the conclusion that he should be ruling Europe. But the principles of logic are principles of reasoning about the real world.

If we discard logic, we have only unprincipled assertion, the force of which depends upon the brute strength (or weapons) of the person staking his claim. If you wish to *demonstrate* logic's inadequacy, you must make your demonstration in a logical way. Your own mind will demand it, as will your conversation partner.

There are excellent books that will teach you the science of logic, and I heartily recommend these as preparation for the work of an apologist or evangelist. It's a matter of charity for us to meet our dialogue partners on common ground; and logic is a necessary component of any relationship that is dia-logic. For this book, however, I wish to cover just four brief points—four propositions that are universally accepted as true, and are practically undeniable. As such, they are the best starting points for dialogue or argument over God's existence.

I. **The principle of non-contradiction.** This is a fairly simple concept, though it's hard to state it simply. Something (let's call it *A*) cannot be both *A* and *not A* at the same time and in the same way. Contradictions are nonsense. I cannot be Scott Hahn and not Scott Hahn. Or to use Aristotle's example: a certain road could not be the road to Megara and, at the same time, *not* be the road to Megara. Some ancients tried to play with words and say that all propositions were simultaneously true and false. But Aristotle observed that these philosophers could not live their lives that way. They would still take the road to Megara when they wanted to reach the city of Megara. Moreover, when they denied the law of non-contradiction, their denial presumed its validity. After all, they assumed the *unequivocal truth* of their own statement denying the very possibility of an unequivocally true statement about reality. Their statement is self-destructive because things just cannot *be* that way.

2. **The general reliability of sense perception.** Our senses correspond to reality as it exists independent of our perceptions. If someone tells you your senses are unreliable, ask him how he knows it. And if he appeals to optical illusions or auditory illusions to show that the senses can be deceived, point out that we know those optical illusions to be *illusions* only because some other sense overrides the sense that's deceived, or our reason discovers the cause of the illusion. If a pencil stuck in a glass of water appears to be bent, we know that it's not because we run our fingers along the length of the pencil and our fingers find it intact. This difference between what the two senses "report" jolts our reason into discovering the laws of optics. We trust our sense of touch and allow it to override the initial misapprehension of the sense of sight. We trust our reason to discover why the senses can sometimes seem to misrepresent what is really there. Sense perception is *generally* reliable. Reason makes up for the deficit. But it is as foolish to reject the senses because they sometimes seem to deceive us as it is to reject mathematics because we sometimes make mistakes in our checkbooks.

3. **The principle of causality.** For every effect, there must be a cause. By "effect" I mean any contingent, finite, or changing thing, and I lay aside questions about the strange subatomic world that seems, to some, to violate this law. We want to focus on the level of reality in which we live and act, and on this everyday level even the "subatomic" physicist lives and acts according to the law of causality. This law underlies both the working of logic and of sense perception. We see flowers, chocolates, and then a kiss, and we conclude that there is a causal relationship at work. Scientists of necessity must assume every effect they are

investigating has a cause, for otherwise they would have nothing to explain and they could explain nothing. If someone argued against causality, once again he would be presenting a self-destructive argument—hoping to cause a change in your mind!

4. **The notion of self-consciousness.** This is what tells me that I exist. I may believe that everything is an illusion, but still I am left with myself—the entity that is entertaining the illusion. Self-consciousness presumes that there is a self, whatever that self may be. I know that I exist, even if I try to pretend that I am uncertain about everything else.

There is much more to logic than these four points, but you can count these among the most important feathers (so to speak) on reason's wing. They make it possible for reason to take flight.

A Mind for What Matters

Even if we can agree on some basic terms, however, we may encounter other apparent obstacles, but sometimes these are easily overcome. Some people, for example, describe themselves as *materialists, objectivists,* or *empiricists.* These tendencies need not be obstacles to dialogue, even though they seem to banish all things spiritual from discourse. In fact, it's far easier to dialogue with these people than with more radical skeptics, like those who doubt the very notion of reality. With the former group, we can at least agree on the importance of material reality, objective reality, and empirical reality. Christians are at ease in creation, because our Father God created the world and all that's in it.

As for those who do not believe that reality exists outside the mind—well, what can you say, if you yourself are just part of the illusion? The philosopher George Berkeley tried to argue for the nonexistence of matter. Samuel Johnson kicked a stone and said: "Thus I refute thee." Johnson was demonstrating the general reliability of sense perception. Or more dramatically, there's the character in one of Hilaire Belloc's novels. After hearing a self-absorbed skeptic at a pub drone on far too long, he threw a beer in his face and shouted, "I baptize thee in the name of the five senses!" It's all well and good to say that reality exists only in one's mind, but those who believe it should still look both ways before crossing the street.

But let's return to the materialists, objectivists, and empiricists. What we need to demonstrate to skeptics is that human beings naturally reason from the visible to the invisible, from the sensible to the insensible. It is something characteristically human. We do it from the time we're babies. An infant encounters certain fluids, and warmth, and high-pitched sounds, and he associates them together, first in the concept "mother," and later in the word "Mama." We see letters and recognize that they represent sounds. We gather the letters into words that represent things that we see around us. We count things from the time we are small, but numbers themselves are immaterial abstractions, and the most hard-headed scientist uses these abstractions all the time.

Most people, too, recognize the need for some immaterial moral principles as well: justice, fairness, freedom, love, compassion, solidarity, and so on. These are abstractions, manifested in concrete events, but not exhausted by those events. We measure the material manifestations against the abstract ideal we hold in our minds.

Music and art, too, move us from the sensory to the abstract. Most people who listen to a Mozart composition will conclude that its thousands of variations in pitch add up to something, evoke something, stand for something greater. The sounds of Mozart move us from the sensible to the abstract, the sensible to the insensible. Aesthetic experiences are not important to everyone, but they can be a profound mystery to an unbeliever who is open to their power, a spiritual foot in the materialist's door.

Materialists, objectivists, and empiricists may be well on their way to the kingdom. As we show them the layers of the universe—even in the natural order—we are preparing them to understand the sacramentality of creation. As the poet Gerard Manley Hopkins said: "The world is charged with the grandeur of God."

TRUST, BUT VERIFY

It is entirely rational, then, for us to reason from the visible to the invisible. In fact, this is what scientists do all the time. Physicist John Polkinghorne once noted: "No one has ever seen a quark, and we believe that no one ever will. They are so tightly bound to each other inside the protons and neutrons that nothing can make them break out on their own. Why, then, do I believe in these invisible quarks? . . . [B]ecause quarks make sense of a lot of direct physical experience, such as the patterns in which particles can be grouped, and the strange way in which projectiles, like electrons, bounce back from collisions with protons and neutrons, just as if there were some tough and tiny constituents sitting inside." He went on to list other unseen phenomena in which he firmly believed, including black holes, pulsars, and quasars.

Now, not all scientists are as eager as Polkinghorne to acknowledge what Polanyi called the fiduciary aspect of their work. Nor will the most brilliant scientists necessarily be the most reasonable and logical thinkers. The physicist Robert March once wrote of old age as the time "when good physicists often turn into bad philosophers." Nevertheless, we can certainly show profound respect for these scientists' achievements and intelligence, without attributing infallibility to them in all matters. We might respectfully point out that they obey the laws of logic even if they deny the validity of those laws, and that they practice a sort of faith, even if they dismiss religious faith as superstition. The question that should remain is whether religious faith, and specifically Catholic faith, is indeed unreasonable. And, as I pointed out earlier, there has always been an impressive array of scientists to attest to Christianity's persuasive power.

These are men and women who soar with both wings—as we want to do. If we want to be true to our human nature, we should eagerly seek to develop our faith and reason. The historian Etienne Gilson described the well-rounded thinker as someone "who does not like to believe what he can know, and who never pretends to know what can be but believed, and yet a man whose faith and knowledge grow into an organic unity because they both spring from the same divine source."

So faith, in a sense, depends upon reason—not in the way that water depends upon hydrogen, but more in the way that each spouse depends upon the other in the home. It is possible for one spouse to go it alone, but the task is difficult and always a struggle. In the same way, it is possible for either faith or reason to struggle mightily and drag us much of the way to understanding, but that's not the way of human nature.

Faith and reason are indeed interdependent. One of the great secrets of the universe is that reason leans on faith every bit as much as faith leans on reason. Rightly did St. Augustine say, "I believe that I may understand." It's not that people who lack Christian faith cannot know anything. But anyone who knows anything must first put faith in principles that are tacit, unproven, and unprovable. We have good reasons for believing such things. But we don't have proof. We believe that we may understand.

Believer or not, anyone who tries to fly on one wing will inevitably fall into one excess or another. The Catholic Church condemns both the disordered reliance on faith alone (*fideism*) and the disordered reliance on reason alone (*rationalism*).

"For we walk by faith, not by sight," St. Paul said (2 Cor 5:7). But that doesn't make it a virtue for us to cross the street with our eyes closed. God made our eyes, and He made them that we might see.

Three

NATURAL REASONS

On the Persuasive Power of the Universe

In the last chapter, I invoked the physicist John Polkinghorne, who described his faith in unseen particles and events, like quarks and quasars. These hypothetical phenomena are the best ways he has found to make sense of the strange phenomena he can see, like the movement of electrons. Polkinghorne believes that it is possible "to engage in a similar strategy with regard to the unseen reality of God. His existence makes sense of many aspects of our knowledge and experience." He holds that "science and religion are intellectual cousins under the skin. Both are searching for motivated belief."

When we explain and defend the faith, we are trying to help develop that motivation. That's why we give *reasons* to believe. That's why St. Peter urges us to give "an account for the hope" that is in us. Those reasons, that account, might provide sufficient motives for belief; so that our hearers might give the assent of faith.

Polkinghorne is affirming the possibility of "natural theology." Natural theology is the branch of philosophy that treats of God's existence and attributes by means of reason, without relying on the

authority of Scripture, tradition, or the Church. While Polkinghorne is a Christian, some of his non-Christian colleagues have
joined him in the pursuit of natural theology. Again, in the last
chapter I mentioned Paul Davies, who wrote about design in creation (*The Cosmic Blueprint*). His work complements that of Sir Fred
Hoyle, a Cambridge don who wrote (in books like *The Intelligent
Universe*) of an apparent "anthropic principle" in the universe—
that is, that the cosmos seems to have been designed so that it
might be perceived by humankind. Another Christian, Arthur Pea-
cocke, in *God and the New Biology* and many other books, has made a
similarly reasoned study of the evidence from living organisms.

These scientists searched for, and found, what Polkinghorne
called "motivated belief." Yet we will sometimes find Christians
who dismiss efforts to know God by means of reason. Such Christians sometimes dismiss natural theology as "unspiritual"—or
even condemn it as an act of spiritual pride and arrogance, the
transgression of the mythological Prometheus, who stole fire from
the gods. It's not that these Christians are radically anti-intellectual
(though some are). In fact, some theologians hold this opinion,
and they assert that God so utterly transcends creation that His existence can be known only through direct acts of self-revelation—
either through the intervention of grace or through the divinely
inspired words of the Bible.

But this position is itself diametrically opposed to the teaching
of Scripture! St. Paul wrote: "Ever since the creation of the world
[God's] invisible nature, namely, His eternal power and deity, has
been clearly perceived in the things that have been made" (Rom
1:20). God Himself is invisible, yet "clearly" perceptible in visible
creation.

St. Paul firmly established the possibility of natural theology,
which had already been practiced for centuries by philosophers of

the schools of Plato and Aristotle. The Church's early apologists often built their own arguments upon the foundations laid by the ancient pagan philosophers. So natural theology is certainly possible. It's been proven effective and persuasive since long before Christ. It is, moreover, confirmed as a method by the clear teaching of the Catholic Church. In fact, it is heresy to deny the possibility of natural theology. The First Vatican Council put the matter in no uncertain terms: "Holy mother Church holds and teaches that God, the source and end of all things, can be known with certainty from the consideration of created things, by the natural power of human reason . . . If anyone says that the one, true God, our creator and lord, cannot be known with certainty from the things that have been made, by the natural light of human reason: let him be anathema."

If God is knowable, then, by the natural light of reason, it's fair to ask why He should bother to reveal anything about Himself through extraordinary or supernatural means. Isn't He just encouraging our laziness? St. Thomas Aquinas faced this problem squarely, noting God's kindness in revealing Himself anyway. For, if the matter were left up to human reason, few people would ever attain the knowledge of God, because the majority would lack either the time, the freedom, or the intellectual capacity. Also, whatever truth they did attain would always be mixed up with error, because even the most well-endowed human reason is still imperfect.

So revelation serves to correct and perfect what we might discover from reason. Revelation also discloses divine truths, such as the dogma of the Trinity, whose reason surpasses human capacities altogether. We'll come back to that idea later. But, for now, let us praise reason, which God has made after the likeness of His own Word, our logic after his Logos. The order in creation is a suitable object for our orderly minds, which themselves, in a mysterious way, reflect the order in the mind of God.

There remains one other group that argues against the use of natural theology. They are sometimes called "fideists" (from the Latin *fides*, meaning "faith"). Fideists claim that God's existence and attributes can be grasped only by faith—and not by reason—because God's existence and attributes are transcendent realities. Some fideists go so far as to say that the pursuit of natural theology is a sign of intellectual or spiritual pride, a pandering to autonomous reason.

One particular type of fideism is called presuppositionalism. Christians from this school have a slightly different approach to the apprehension of God's existence. They hold that everyone, deep down, already has faith in God. It's an unspoken, often unacknowledged part of the human package. All human thought, speech, and action (they argue) presupposes a belief in God, whose existence makes all subsequent order possible. Why, then, do we meet professing atheists and agnostics? Because, according to the fideists and presuppositionalists, some people live in a persistent state of denial about the faith that they hold deep down. While presuppositionalists usually place a low value on natural theology, some will concede that there's no harm in showing people what they already know and giving them greater certainty in a matter of which they're only dimly aware.

After all, maybe some of those tacit believers might even move beyond their state of denial.

Let us look, then, at some of the ways the human mind might proceed (or be led) in an orderly fashion, to reach motivated and reasonable belief in the existence of God.

PROOFS POSITIVE

Down through the ages, philosophers and saints have put forth various demonstrations of the existence of God. Some people call these "proofs" or "arguments." Those of St. Thomas Aquinas are perhaps the most famous, and they are known simply as the "Five Ways." Thomas was not the first to show, from reason and experience, how we know of God's existence and attributes; nor do his Ways exhaust all the possibilities. In fact, Peter Kreeft and Ronald Tacelli offer twenty arguments for God's existence in their *Handbook of Christian Apologetics;* and those, too, are just a representative sampling.

We need, also, to keep in mind that many of the demonstrations for God's existence come to us from a time when philosophers could assume a universal belief in the divine. Through most of history, most sane people affirmed the existence of some divinity. They may have declared themselves agnostic about the divine nature or attributes; but they acknowledged the necessary existence of a god or gods. This was as true of non-Christians as of Christians. St. Thomas built his Five Ways upon the foundations of Aristotle and Plato, both pagan Greeks who lived four centuries before Jesus Christ. They (and not Scripture) were his primary authorities in showing how we can come to know God's existence. In the ancient world, the word *atheism* denoted the denial of the orthodox God (or gods). It was not until the nineteenth century that anyone seriously proposed the denial of any divinity at all; and such a denial indeed requires an immense leap of faith—certainly no less than belief in any traditional notion of God.

The existence of God is at least reasonable—if not "self-evident," as America's founding fathers believed—and good rea-

sons are generally what we find in the so-called proofs or demonstrations. All demonstrations are reducible either to direct sensory
experience ("seeing is believing") or so-called *quia* proofs, that is,
arguments reasoning backward from evidence, from effects to a
necessary cause of those effects, as a team of detectives might make
at the scene of a crime—reasoning backward to a thief from the
footprints, fingerprints, and other traces he left behind. Since "no
one has ever seen God" (I Jn 4:12), all demonstrations for His existence are *quia* demonstrations.

WAYS TO GO

St. Thomas begins his Five Ways with the "argument from motion." We might also call it an argument from "change" or "development." It proceeds from a simple fact: everything in the world
that we experience and know *undergoes change*, proceeding from the
potential to the actual. Everything moves or changes. Yet nothing
moves or changes itself. Everything that moves must be moved by
something already in motion. But this chain of motion cannot
regress infinitely. An infinite chain of movers would not suffice to
explain the motion. It must have a beginning that is unmoved. The
unmoved prime mover is what we call God.

Consider an analogy: imagine that you drive up to a railroad
crossing, only to find a train passing by. You see boxcar after boxcar after boxcar, first dozens of them and then hundreds of them.
You arrived as the train was already in motion, so you never saw the
engine. But you must infer that the train has an engine; because, if
you see a train in motion, you know that something is moving it.
An engine is pulling it. If you try to solve the problem by positing
an infinite series of boxcars, you haven't done away with the need
for explaining the motion. You've enlarged the problem—*infinitely*.

If you deny the existence of the engine, then you've enlarged the need to find a much bigger and extraordinary cause for the motion of such a long line of boxcars.

The train analogy casts light upon St. Thomas's second Way as well: the argument from efficient causality. This argument is similar to the first. It begins by noting that every effect has a cause. Still, the causal chain cannot be infinite any more than the chain of motion can. Yet neither can any cause in the sequence be considered an ultimate beginning; because, if we deny that first effect its own cause, we would nullify all the subsequent effects. We cannot have an infinite regress in causes, so we must posit an uncaused first cause, and that first cause is what we call God.

The third Way is based on possibility and necessity. We observe that things are transitory; they receive their existence from something else. The things we see in the world do not arise suddenly out of nothing, but rather are derivative of other things, contingent upon the existence of other things. Yet, again, an infinite chain of derivation is unthinkable, absurd. It's not enough to propose an infinite series of beings that, each and all, require a cause. If some beings are contingent, there must be an ultimate being that is neither transitory nor derivative, but necessary—necessary in and of itself. And it is that being we call God.

In the first three Ways, St. Thomas presented cosmological arguments. He reasoned from physical evidence. In the next two Ways, he shifts gears a bit, and he moves from the cosmological to the teleological, from a consideration of origins to a consideration of ends and purposes.

The fourth Way considers the "degrees of perfection." St. Thomas observes that we all judge certain things to have a greater or lesser degree of perfection than others. We say something is more or less true, more or less good, and so on. Such relative measurements imply an absolute standard of measurement. A tape measure must mark the distance between two end points. Its degrees—whether inches, feet, yards, or miles—must be marked relative to some constant and absolute standard. This is true of all qualities. But there must be some perfect standard against which all qualities are measured. That fullness of all perfection we call God.

The fifth Way is the "argument from design" or "finality" (in other words, "intelligent action"). St. Thomas begins by noting that things that lack any intelligence still act in a purposeful way. They seem to have specific ends and observe certain patterns, certain "laws" of the universe—the laws of gravity, thermodynamics, and so on—and these many laws all seem to work together in an orderly manner. If we update this proof with modern physics, we must stand in awe of a cosmos that functions in a relatively stable and predictable way, in spite of the apparently erratic occurrences that take place constantly at the subatomic level. Even the various theories of evolution—which some commentators have tried to place in opposition to intelligent design—actually only confirm the fifth Way. For Charles Darwin as for Thomas Aquinas, nature observed certain ironclad laws and pursued certain purposes in an orderly and predictable manner. Even in Darwinism, nature observes a process of selection; the fittest survive. All of this implies purpose, order, standards, and ends.

Even unintelligent things function in a way that reflects an ordered purpose. There is a design. And if there is a design, there must be a designer.

Consider an analogy: You're walking along the beach, and you see something glimmer in the sun. You reach down and pick it up—a small, circular metal object with a glass-covered face. You note that it makes a ticking noise, and you see that, behind the glass, it is composed of gears, springs, screws, and markings for measurement. All the pieces are precisely and delicately fitted together. Well, what is that object? And how did it come into existence? Could it be the result of countless waves pounding the seashore, grinding shells to dust—dust that is then reconfigured by the wind into this particular configuration that moves so precisely?

Is the human intellect capable of imagining that kind of process? Yes, but it's implausible. In a similar way, when you study creation, you see evidence for design, and design points to a designer. The eye is a system of irreducible complexity, composed of a retina, cornea, lens, vitreous humor, and aqueous humor. It cannot simply be the result of an arbitrary process. The eye is made with a certain design, made for the purpose of seeing; and each of its parts assumes the functioning of all the other parts. What good would an antecedent organ have served in any hypothetical earlier stages—before the organ could see? It would be no good at all. The eye is made with an end in mind: to see. This is true for everything else, from subatomic particles and cells to solar systems and galaxies. The empirical sciences themselves are possible only because the universe is orderly, patterned, symmetrical, observable, and (to some degree at least) measurable and predictable.

We may reasonably conclude that the device on the beach had a manufacturer, and that the manufacturer had a purpose in mind when making it. A watch requires a watchmaker. In a similar way, an ordered universe requires the existence of an intelligent creator; and we call that creator God.

OTHER WAYS

As I noted earlier, St. Thomas is not the only thinker to propose demonstrations of God's existence. In fact, the German philosopher Immanuel Kant rejected all of St. Thomas's arguments, but conceived one of his own, which is sometimes called the "moral argument." This line of thinking was developed further by Venerable John Henry Newman in the nineteenth century, and then put concisely by C. S. Lewis in the twentieth.

These men argue that human beings observe a universal standard of right and wrong. Every people on earth, and every culture in history, has praised the virtue of courage and condemned the vice of cowardice. There are no ancient epics honoring men who abandoned their comrades in battle. Such universality extends to norms in other areas of life as well. Another example: though tribes differ about the particulars of sexual morality, there has never been a society that placed no restraints whatsoever on human sexuality.

This universal moral sense—call it conscience—requires a standard by which people judge questions of justice. Morals cannot be simply a matter of personal preference. Very few people are willing to accept serial killing or serial rape as an alternative lifestyle.

Yet any condemnation of these actions requires the acknowledgment of some fixed, universal standard. Any recognition of transcultural human rights and duties requires that we acknowledge those rights and duties as decreed by an ultimate authority. And that authority we call God.

Another famous argument about God's existence is not really a demonstration at all, but rather a bet. It is known as "Pascal's Wager," after the noted mathematician Blaise Pascal. It is not so much an argument for the *existence* of God as an argument for *faith* in God. Pascal, whose specialty was probability, was simply applying decision theory to ultimate questions.

Pascal considers God's existence in terms of a coin toss. Either God exists or He doesn't. "Let us weigh up the gain and the loss involved in calling heads that God exists. Let us assess the two cases: if you win you win everything, if you lose you lose nothing. Do not hesitate then; wager that He does exist."

His actual argument runs longer than that; and, to be fair, Pascal composed the Wager not for publication, but as a note to himself. Like many other people, I have not found his argument persuasive. In fact, it's fairly easy to poke fun at it. For example: what if there exists a deity who frowns upon gambling, especially over the state of His existence?

I feel compelled, however, to include Pascal's Wager for the simple historical fact that it has persuaded so many people—including two of my friends, both of them professional philosophers! For that reason alone, I'm willing to bet on its usefulness.

There are other fascinating approaches to God. Some apologists posit an argument from history. They note that human events seem to coalesce into a story line, a great narrative, and that the plot indicates providential oversight, which could come only from God.

Still others put forth an "argument from desire," noting that every human longing finds fulfillment in a real object. Hunger is satisfied by food. Thirst is quenched by water. The sex drive finds satiety in married love. Yes, as C. S. Lewis noted, human beings long for something that nothing in the world can satisfy, and that is because we were created for another world.

Finally, I cannot help but include Kreeft and Tacelli's version of the argument from aesthetic experience:

There is the music of Johann Sebastian Bach.
Therefore there must be a God.

They conclude with the caveat: "You either see this one or you don't."

That "argument" always brings a smile to my face—but it's not a joke. Great beauty elevates the soul, and the literature of conversion is replete with testimony from those whose hearts were truly moved to faith by the works of Bach, and Michelangelo, and Dante, and the romances of the Holy Grail.

Plato spoke of four transcendentals: the one, the true, the good, and the beautiful. Any of these paths can take our friends above and beyond the everyday; and from there they might see their way clear to God.

Persuasions Remain Invitations

These Ways and means of natural theology are essential exercises for any Christian who wants to take up the challenge of explaining or defending the faith today. Natural theology helps us to meet atheists, agnostics, and other nonbelievers on the common ground of the cosmos and the human nature we share—and to help them see how God has disclosed His existence and attributes "in the things that have been made" (Rom 1:20).

The Ways are not proofs, really, at least not in the sense we understand the word "proof" today. They are, in fact, more than proofs. They are ways of knowing God, of recognizing His primacy in all orders of value, of acknowledging Him most clearly as our origin and guide. Yet no demonstration can force the intellect or the will to take the next step: the act of faith. The Ways lead us to rational belief about God's existence and attributes. But Christ's divinity remains another sort of thing—it is a matter of faith.

St. Thomas Aquinas emphasized that his demonstrations were merely *invitations* to belief and not formal reasons for assenting to faith. The great Dominican theologian Romanus Cessario wrote, "Even Christ's miracles or other supernatural phenomena fall short of providing proportionate evidence for the judgmental assent of faith." If even Jesus' miracles could not force an absolutely conclusive case, we should not expect too much from our own argumentative skills.

We cannot impose orthodox conclusions on our unbelieving friends. To borrow words from Benjamin Franklin: The mind changed against the will is of the same opinion still. God endowed every human being with freedom, and we are always free to choose unbelief. Such a choice is a sad use of freedom. It's like a railroad train jumping the tracks in order to be free of them, and then being unable ever to move again.

Yet people can choose *not* to think rationally. They can choose to violate the laws of the mind. They can even use the laws of the mind while they're denying those very laws. We can't force people to stop. In fact, we can force them away if we come on too forcefully. I know of many people who didn't believe in God, and were actually further repelled, the more people argued with them.

That's why humility, prayer, and love are the most essential arguments for the apologist. As St. Peter put it: "do so with gentleness and reverence" (I Pet 3:15). If we truly love people, we've got to love them where they are. And if they're not sure of God's existence, it does no good for us to tell them, "Just believe anyway, step out into the darkness." No, we should have enough confidence to ask them to step out into the light. Still, the light can be overwhelming to someone who's been sitting in darkness, and it may take some time for them to see.

Four

RIGHT AND WRONG

On Doing and Denial

Every culture agrees, in general terms, that good is to be done and evil avoided. In the last chapter I alluded to the universality of certain moral norms, and I mentioned courage and cowardice as examples of traits that are everywhere—and without exception—recognized, respectively, as a virtue and a vice. You and I could multiply other examples. Most cultures condemn most forms of murder and theft.

Now, some people might argue that these behaviors are commonplace today and even tacitly approved in modern Western society. Many people cheat on their spouses, pilfer office supplies, falsify tax returns, and even arrange for the destruction of their unborn babies. Do these people really believe that they're doing the wrong thing?

The answer, I believe, is yes. They do, at some level, know that they're doing wrong. I acknowledge that some people tell lies, even habitually; but even the most egregious liars do not want people to lie to them. Many people commit adultery; but even the most notorious lothario does not want to be betrayed in turn. Tax evaders do not want to be cheated by others. And no abortionist wants the instruments of his trade to be turned against his own limbs and vital organs. So even those who act against the most basic moral precepts bear witness to those same precepts by their own personal aversions and by their deepest sense of justice. They may not behave justly, but they want others to act justly toward them.

It is no accident that murder, theft, lying, and adultery are among the sins prohibited by the Ten Commandments, the essence of the law that God gave to Moses on Mount Sinai. But there is nothing special about these laws, nothing peculiarly "Jewish" or "Christian" about them. They are universal, and even the prophets of Israel recognized that fact. Isaiah and Amos inveighed against the gentile nations because they held gentiles accountable to those same basic standards, and so judged them to be guilty of grave transgressions.

Some people do try to raise doubts about the possibility of universal moral norms. Yet their very arguments, like the arguments against logic we discussed in chapter 2, are self-refuting. They say, for example, that "there are no absolutes"—yet that itself is an absolute statement! Or they say, "You should never impose your morality on other people"—which is itself a moral prescription! In rejecting morality, people must paradoxically embrace a morality that is opposite and equally imposing.

Other opponents will take a different and more subtle approach. They'll start by citing so-called "hard cases," moral decisions involving ambiguous and extenuating circumstances. But that is a poor place to begin. Religious moralists, too, will recognize all those factors in determining a person's guilt or innocence.

The gray areas will always provoke debate. We should acknowledge, however, that there are actions that evoke an unqualified response of horror. I have yet to meet anyone who contends that the torture of children is a matter of moral indifference. A person who would advocate that position might rightly be judged insane; for our standards of sanity imply that certain thoughts are natural and others are mad, certain thoughts are human and others are not. The acceptance of child torture is deeply unnatural.

And, when people visit the death camps of Auschwitz or Birkenau—or when they read about the killing fields of Cambodia, or tribal genocide in Rwanda—they don't just smile and say, "Those perpetrators had values so different from my own. This world is wonderfully diverse!" No, they say, "This is evil." No one needs to carry out a cost-benefit analysis before passing judgment on mass murder and sadism. The blood of the victims seems to cry out from the ground for justice.

People will usually recognize evil, even if they are reluctant to recognize good. Some might look at an apparently heroic action and imagine a selfish motive behind it—the desire for fame, or praise, or monetary reward. Few people, however, will hesitate to call evil by its name.

Yet, once they have done so, they have placed themselves in a bind. Indeed, they have bound themselves by law. Because evil is possible only as the *perversion* of something good, the *opposite* of something good, the *denial* of something good. Once people have judged something evil, they have acknowledged a transcendent standard of good. They themselves have placed the world under a law.

Nor can they escape the bind by saying that law exists, but merely as a utilitarian stopgap, to ensure the safety of the greatest number of people. For even then they are invoking transcendent standards: the notion, for example, that the common good is greater than the individual good; or that anyone should be concerned with another person's safety. Utilitarianism cannot suffice to prevent murder or theft, because some individuals sometimes find these actions quite useful.

Yet they are actions universally condemned, by civil law and common morals. Such condemnations are among the moral truths that human beings *naturally* know. These norms witness to something that philosophers describe as the "natural law."

HEARTWRITING

The natural law is not only universally human; it is distinctively human. It is consonant with the "law of nature" that governs the movements of nonhuman creatures; but it is not identical with that law, because for other creatures, law is inexorable. Gravity, for example, cannot be disobeyed. Neither can animal instinct. Humans, however, have the power of choice; they can choose certain actions and avoid others. According to the natural law, they should do good and avoid evil.

My friend Russell Hittinger calls the natural law "the first grace," because it is every human being's direct participation in God's eternal law. It comes with the basic equipment of our creation "in God's image" (Gen 1:26–27). St. Paul, in his Letter to the Romans, said that the righteous gentiles "do by nature what the law requires [and] are a law to themselves, even though they do not have the law" (Rom 2:14). The pagans do not know God's special revelation to Israel; yet "what the law requires is written on their hearts" (v. 15).

That's why people in every time and place have been able to appeal to a common sense of justice. That's why people in every time and place have shown admiration for the same basic set of virtues and abhorrence of the same basic set of vices.

The natural law is a beautiful reality, an empirically verifiable fact of creation. Together with natural theology, it is accessible to everyone as a kind of "natural religion."

But it is fair to ask, again, why a world equipped with such a religious sense should need a supernatural revelation. And why, too, if the entire human race is so equipped, is the world in such a moral and religious muddle?

Earlier in his Letter to the Romans, St. Paul anticipates these questions. He establishes what can be known about God by reason alone: "Ever since the creation of the world His invisible nature, namely, His eternal power and deity, has been clearly perceived in the things that have been made" (Rom 1:20). But with that sure knowledge came a natural obligation of praise and worship; and it is this obligation that people neglected: "for although they knew God they did not honor Him as God or give thanks to Him" (v. 21). This failure had the effect of pulling down the blinds against the sunlight: "they became futile in their thinking and their senseless minds were darkened. Claiming to be wise, they became fools" (vv. 21–22).

The gentiles' refusal to worship began a spiral of sin. Sin, in turn, further darkened the intellect and eclipsed even the attributes of God that could be known by nature. Yet humankind is by nature religious, and so people turned to worship what they loved most: the things of the world. They "exchanged the glory of the immortal God for images resembling mortal man or birds or animals or reptiles" (Rom 1:23). It's not that they worshiped *bad things*; men and birds and reptiles are good creatures of God. But they do not suffice as objects of worship. We should worship God alone, in whose image we are made. When people begin to worship anything less than God—even if they worship the crown of His creation—they begin to degrade themselves. They refashion not only their worship, but themselves as well. As they worship, so they live, now imitating animal instinct rather than any truly human morality.

And God respects their decision: "Therefore God gave them up in the lusts of their hearts to impurity, to the dishonoring of their bodies among themselves because they exchanged the truth about God for a lie and worshiped and served the creature rather than the Creator" (vv. 24–25).

Paul goes on to describe the downward spiral of sin, as he recounts how so many people "by their wickedness suppress the truth" (v. 18). In Paul's view, immorality and unbelief are codependent dispositions. People must ignore or deny God if they want to do things that are objectively wrong. And as these actions become habitual, so does their ignorance or denial of God.

Paul does not treat atheism as an intellectual problem. He assumes that God is knowable and known. He assumes that people know, quite naturally, the difference between right and wrong.

No, Paul treats atheism as a problem of the heart and will—a failure of nerve. People want their way, and atheism is the price they pay for insisting on having their way.

Nevertheless, if atheism is not *at root* an intellectual problem, it manifests many intellectual symptoms; and we have to treat the symptoms if we want to eradicate the problem. So it's necessary for us to develop proofs for God's existence and for the existence of the natural law—effectively closing in on the problem from both sides.

THE FATHER OF INVENTION?

I have to admit: It was a contrarian student who helped me to see this matter clearly.

Once, in the classroom, while I was expounding on St. Thomas's

Five Ways, a young guy named John raised his hand and said, "You know what I think, Professor Hahn?" He hardly paused before saying, "I think that, if God *didn't* exist, we'd invent Him anyway. And we *did*. What do you say to that?"

He was asking a hard question. What, after all, can we say to people who dismiss our idea of God as merely a pleasant fantasy?

Then, rather suddenly, I remembered that passage from St. Paul's Letter to the Romans, and I knew how I should answer.

"You know what I say, John? I say, if God *did* exist, we'd invent *atheism* anyway. And we did."

John raised an eyebrow. He was surprised.

"John," I said, "I don't know what you're like, but I know what I'm like. And I know what God is like—at least the God I say I believe in. That God is infinite; and He's all-wise, so He knows everything about me. He's all-good, too, and all righteous, and perfectly holy. And He commands me to be perfectly holy, too. Since He's all-wise, he knows exactly when I'm not very holy or good, and He judges me based on what He knows. Oh, and He's immutable, too, so He'll never change. He'll always be the way He is now; so He'll always hold the same standards; and He's always going to judge me by every idle word I utter."

I could tell by John's expression that he saw where I was going. I continued: "I have to admit, John, that *that* kind of God threatens my present state of existence and my lifestyle. If I were going to invent a god, I'd probably make one more congenial to my whims. And if I didn't have the sense to invent him that way in the first place, I'd at least invent a god who could change his mind."

John had simply repeated a slogan the modern world learned from Ludwig Feuerbach in the nineteenth century. Feuerbach believed that human beings invented God because they needed a crutch and a consolation. God was their substitute for reason—a projection of their irrational desires in the face of inevitable death. The idea of God was, in Feuerbach's view, especially useful to men who possessed power and authority, who were only too eager to use a divine mandate to justify their agenda. "God" was the wily monarch's way of keeping the ignorant and superstitious rabble on their best behavior.

To discredit Feuerbach's ideas, it might be enough to point out that they profoundly influenced two other thinkers, Karl Marx and Friedrich Nietzsche, who were in turn the forerunners of communism and Nazism, two ideologies both godless and deadly. It was Feuerbach who made Stalin and Hitler possible, because he assured them that they acted in the absence of God. And, as we learned from Feuerbach's contemporary, the novelist Fyodor Dostoyevsky, "If God does not exist, then everything is permitted"—everything, even murder on an epic scale. It turned out that godlessness was a much more useful weapon in the hands of a despot than God ever had been—even the fantasy "God" imagined by Feuerbach.

Ideologues first fabricated God's absence. Then they acted as if it were true. Their denial of even natural theology permitted them to flout the natural law with impunity. Their rejection of natural law, in turn, closed off reason's natural pathway to God.

But nature reveals God the lawgiver as well as God the creator. Every human being has to come to grips with that, or live with the consequences: "And since they did not see fit to acknowledge God, God gave them up to a base mind and to improper conduct. They were filled with all manner of wickedness, evil, covetousness, malice. Full of envy, murder, strife, deceit, malignity, they are gossips, slanderers, haters of God, insolent, haughty, boastful, inventors of evil, disobedient to parents, foolish, faithless, heartless, ruthless. Though they know God's decree that those who do such things deserve to die, they not only do them but approve those who practice them" (Rom 1:28–32).

My student John was surely wrong, but it was his boldness that helped me understand the profound logic of St. Paul's argument. If human beings had really tried to invent a god, we would *never* have invented the God of Christianity. He's just too terrifying. Our God is all-powerful, all-knowing, all-holy, and omnipresent. There's no place to run and hide from Him, no place where we might secretly indulge a favorite vice. We can't even retreat into the dark corners of our minds to *fantasize* about that vice without God knowing it right away.

Such a God makes any violation of the natural law a very uncomfortable business. If determined sinners could find a way to dispel such a notion of God, imagine their feeling of liberation. If your imagination fails you, then try reading the history of the wars and genocides of the atheist regimes of the twentieth century: Nazi Germany, Communist China and Cambodia, and the Soviet Union.

THE ONLY PROBLEM

Recent history is indeed an overwhelming chronicle of bloodshed—wholesale slaughter with the speed and efficiency of a modern factory. With St. Paul we say that this is what humankind will do in the pretended absence of God.

But how do we respond to those who cite these evils as evidence of God's *real* absence? What do we say to those who argue that a good God could not have permitted evil to persist—and seemingly prevail, as at Auschwitz and Rwanda and in the killing fields.

The problem of evil is *the* problem. The novelist Muriel Spark referred to it as "the only problem." We study the animal kingdom and see that nature is red in tooth and claw. We turn on the news and see violence, death, and suffering all around the globe. While the arguments against God's existence may not be very persuasive, the arguments against His goodness are, to some people, over-whelming.

How should we respond when people raise the problem of suf-fering? First, we should admit that the problem plagues us, too, and brings us to tears and to prayer. Even St. Paul felt the force of the problem with all his heart and mind. He called it the "mystery of iniquity" (2 Thess 2:7). It is a mystery, something hidden even from so great a saint.

Why is there evil if God is both all-powerful and all-good? If He is all-good, His creation should reflect that perfection. If He is all-powerful, then He should be able to prevent evil from hap-pening.

Yet we cannot solve the problem by dismissing God. In fact, such a denial only makes the problem worse. Denying God's exis-tence in order to solve the problem of evil is like burning your house down in order to get rid of termites, or cutting off your head to stop a nosebleed. People who allow evil to drive them to atheism suddenly have no standard by which to judge something evil. Instead of solving the problem, they've institutionalized it—written it into the very fabric of the cosmos. If there is no God, then there is no transcendent, ultimate goodness, no perfect mea-surement of righteousness; and so there can be no true evil, either. Without God, everything becomes a matter of moral indifference or mere human preference.

Some non-Christian religions claim that both moral and physi-cal evils are just part of the balance of life—like male and female, or light and darkness—and that all these opposites ultimately re-side in God. This view is known as "dualism," and it is one way that people have tried to account for evil amid the good that's in the world. Dualism traces it all back to God, who created the world just the way it is, with all its ups and downs.

That, however, leaves the dualist no better off than the atheist; because, if good and evil are co-ultimate, once again we have no standard by which to judge an action. If good and evil both originate in God, they are morally equal phenomena, and we must accept them on equal terms.

WHAT'S MISSING

But dualism is not a valid Christian understanding, because Christian faith asserts that God made the world and everything in it, and it was good (see Gen 1). There was no admixture of evil in God's original plan. There was no taint in His creation.

To achieve any clarity in the matter, we should first determine what evil is—or rather *isn't*, because Christians believe that evil has no existence of its own. I'm not saying that evil is not real. It is painfully real, but it is always a lack of something good, something that should be present. It is a diminishment, a privation.

We further distinguish between two types of evil: *physical evil* and *moral evil*, because these two present problems are related but not identical.

Physical evil is something negative that happens—sickness, blindness, pain, natural disasters, and death. All are privations. Sickness is the absence of health; blindness is the absence of sight; death is the privation of life; and so on.

Moral evil is something that's done. It is the action of a culpable actor. Moral evil is unrighteousness, wickedness, sin. Moral evil, too, represents a lack, but now a privation of a moral good. Adultery is a lack of fidelity. Lying is the absence of truth. Murder is the taking of life.

Once we establish that evil is not a thing, then we see that it is alien to God's creation; because He made the world and everything in it, but (to put a new emphasis on a familiar Scripture) *"nothing is impossible* with God" (Lk 1:37).

So evil does not originate in God. But we still have to account for its reality and its possibility. For how could a good God permit such privation?

When God made both human beings and angels, he made us rational, free, and capable of loving. This means, however, that we have the possibility of choosing *something other than God.* It was necessary for us to have this choice, because true love cannot be coerced. If we did not have the freedom to say no to God, we could not truly love Him. Thus, God could not create a species with free choice without also permitting the possibility of evil.

To move beyond this problem, we need to move from the philosophical to the theological, from reason to revelation, because iniquity is a mystery, and it is only by revelation that we can gain any insight into the true mysteries of faith.

FALLING UPWARD INTO MERCY

Why does God permit evil? Again, the doubter will observe that God must not be all-good, or else His creation would reflect that perfection; He must not be all-powerful, or else He would have fixed the problem by now.

But what if God were able to use evil to show forth His infinite goodness and power? What if, through an act of salvation, He could bring about a greater good than would have been possible, apart from the reality of evil?

If you've ever attended the Easter Vigil liturgy of the Latin Rite, then you've heard the ancient hymn with the line "O happy fault!

O necessary sin of Adam!" Well, did it make you wonder why the Church would celebrate a sin and a fault as "happy"?

As great as unfallen human nature could be, it could not compare to what God has given us in Christ. We might say that God let us break a bone so that He Himself could reset it, making it not just stronger but unbreakable. God has allowed us to lose not only divine grace, but also the standing we had as His servants, His obedient slaves. He foresaw that we would fall. He didn't cause it, but He did freely permit it. He did so in order to bring about a glorious new creation that exceeds every possibility belonging to human nature. So Christ took our fallen human nature, and didn't merely bring it back to life. He united it to Himself, so that the life He restored in us was *divine* life. The grace He gave us was His own sonship.

We share in the divine sonship of Jesus Christ. This is the essence of salvation and the substance of Catholicism. Baptized into Christ, we are partakers of the divine nature (2 Pet 1:4). We live the life of the Blessed Trinity, calling upon Christ's Father as "Our Father." Life doesn't get any better than that, or any more perfect. And none of this would have been possible without the original fall from grace—an event that depended, in turn, upon God's permitting the possibility of evil.

The Gospel, according to the Catholic Church, is more than just a legal declaration of our innocence. It's not just that we stand before God the Father looking like Jesus. We are filled with the very life of God, as much as a creature can be. We could never have achieved this ourselves. That's why God let us fall, in order to let us creatures discover our weakness and dependence, and the greatness of His mercy.

Many people today think that salvation is something God owes us. They don't recognize the gravity of sin, and they don't understand the true purpose of law.

The law of God in all its forms—even the natural law—is a program for our maturity, so that we can pile up habits upon habits. The virtues are nothing but forms of love, which is the essence of the law. Love is manifest in self-giving, self-sacrifice, and self-denial. God is commanding us to an absolute unswerving commitment to holiness, because He knows that our happiness and fulfillment depend upon it. If we obey completely and totally, all we've done is pay the minimum requirement. "We are unworthy servants; we have only done what was our duty" (Lk 17:10).

It isn't that God comes out a richer deity because of what we give Him. The law is not for His sake. Our holiness is not for His gain. It's for us. He gives us the law because of His mercy. Again, because of His mercy, He allows violations of the natural law to have severe consequences. For even the natural law has incentives and disincentives, so that we'll learn from experience to do good and avoid evil. God allows us to suffer, too, because of His mercy. He won't allow us to escape the plan of maturity that even Jesus Christ had to complete.

With eyes of faith, we do not wonder why God allows so much suffering, but rather why He doesn't allow more. We're not looking at a world full of innocent people suffering unjustly. We're looking at a world soaked through with oceans of mercy, because all of us are sinners, and none of us deserves even the next breath we're going to take.

St. Paul put suffering in an eternal perspective: "I consider that the sufferings of this present time are not worth comparing with the glory that is to be revealed to us" (Rom 8:18). For Christ Himself suffered great physical evils and even moral evils at the hands of the people He came to save. If that is our lot, He wanted it to be his lot, too. So, if that was His lot, we should be content with it as our own as well. For "we are children of God, and if children, then heirs, heirs of God and fellow heirs with Christ, *provided we suffer with Him* in order that we may also be glorified with Him" (Rom 8:16–17).

BACK TO NATURE

Even in the natural order, our actions have consequences. The natural law, like all real laws, must decree real penalties. You don't need faith to see that the wages of sin is death. A dissolute lifestyle *dissolves* life. Sinners are miserable people; and there is no life so impoverished as that of a sinner who no longer recognizes his misery. Think, for example, of the drunk in denial, embarrassing himself in the course of another lost evening.

The penalty of the morning after is painful. But God established the penalties of the natural law to be remedial punishments—the discipline of a good Father, who denies His children one thing in order to give them something far better. The hangover should be enough to put the drinker off the drink. If he chooses to ignore the discipline, then his habit will become worse and more severe consequences will surely follow, because his own faculties will grow weaker and will require more drastic measures for correction. This will continue until the poor fellow accepts the mercy of the remedy—a painful moment, but the beginning of a new life. Yet he always remains free. If he declines the mercy, he chooses the means of his own destruction.

The natural law exists in order to prepare human beings for supernatural grace. Grace does not destroy nature, but builds upon it, repairs its every privation, perfects it, and then elevates it.

Some people charge that Christian "supernaturalism" somehow diminishes nature. But it doesn't at all. God made nature good; and the more we realize its goodness, the more that grace will have to build upon. A Christian like St. Paul wished not to overwhelm nature, but to praise it, even as it was manifested in natural law, natural theology, natural religion, and the religious lives of righteous pagans.

This is an important lesson for us to learn and re-learn in every generation. In the mid-1940s, when various peoples of the world met to form the United Nations, they were at first stalled in their discussion because of the diversity of their philosophical, religious, and moral perspectives. How could communists, Christian Democrats, Muslims, and red-blooded Americans even begin to work toward common goals? It took a Catholic philosopher, Jacques Maritain, to lead the nations (or at least their representatives) beyond the philosophical impasse, and the natural law was the means by which he could do it.

Imagine, then, what breakthroughs this language might facilitate in the so-called "culture wars" that divide peoples today.

It is our common nature that gives us a common language for conversation. And it is in this common language that we can begin to proclaim our reasons to believe, especially to the righteous unbelievers we encounter today. Consider the loving approach of St. Paul, as he preached to the Athenians: "Men of Athens, I perceive that in every way you are very religious. For as I passed along, and observed the objects of your worship, I found also an altar with this inscription, 'To an unknown god.' What therefore you worship as unknown, this I proclaim to you—*the God who made the world and everything in it*, the Lord of heaven and earth!" (see Acts 17:22–24).

Five

THE LIMITS OF REASON

On the Testimony of Miracles and Prophecy

We have, till now, dealt mostly with the arguments of people who are skeptical about God's existence or His knowability, skeptical about religion and about morality. Such people need our witness, because they lack the guidance and consolations that true religion can give. If we were going to use triage—if we were to divide our witness the way medical professionals give priority to emergency cases—these skeptics might receive the most intensive care.

Atheists and agnostics, however, make up a relatively small (though growing) portion of the population. The numbers vary from place to place; but in the United States, where I live, and indeed through much of the world, most people admit to some belief in God. They are "theists." Some adhere to the world's non-Christian religions (e.g., Jews and Muslims, Hindus and Sikhs). Others are simply convinced on philosophical grounds that God exists, but have gone no further in their investigations. Some think that a deity is "out there," but also that He is unknowable, remote, and perhaps unaware of the progress of creation.

Many theists are not Christians, and it is important that we strive to help them discover the truth, goodness, beauty—and salvation—that only Christ can give. "The Catholic Church," says the *Catechism*, "recognizes in other religions that search, among shadows and images, for the God who is unknown yet near since He gives life and breath and all things and wants all men to be saved. Thus, the Church considers all goodness and truth found in these religions as a preparation for the Gospel and given by Him who enlightens all men that they may at length have life" (n. 843).

In a sense, our work of evangelization is easier when we speak with theists, since we don't have to persuade them of God's existence or (usually) the basics of morality. They have weighed the evidence and found it convincing. In another sense, though, they present a more difficult challenge, because their next step requires more than an honest intellectual effort. It requires the assent of the will. It takes faith.

Our burden is not to persuade them *that God is*, but rather to persuade them of *who God is*. We worship the God of Abraham and Isaac and Jacob. He is the Word who was made flesh in Jesus Christ. He is the Spirit who descended at creation and at Pentecost. He is the Holy Trinity we invoke in every prayer. He is not something, but Someone. He's not out there, but near to us at all times.

That's a tall order of persuasion, and it sounds like an impossible task. Indeed, it is. We cannot prove *who* God is on merely rational grounds. But we can help persuade people that God has revealed Himself in the history of His people. And if we lead them to encounter Him in His self-revelation, then we have led them as far as we possibly can—and He can certainly take it from there.

Christians have traditionally demonstrated the credibility of

God's revelation in two powerful ways: by means of miracles, and by means of prophecies.

These are the very means that St. Paul evoked for the Christians of Corinth, just a couple of decades after Jesus' ascension. "Jews demand signs," he said, "and Greeks seek wisdom" (I Cor 1:22). Indeed, the Jews at Capernaum had asked Jesus: "Then what sign do You do, that we may see, and believe You? What work do You perform?" (Jn 6:30).

Jesus recognized this very human need for evidence, and so He provided both signs and wisdom. He worked many miracles, for example, which were recorded by eyewitnesses in the Gospels; and miraculous phenomena have continued throughout the history of the Church. Some people consider even *the survival of the Church* to be a first-class miracle! Can you name any other institution that has endured all the vicissitudes of history since the time of the Roman Empire—and prevailed? There is none.

Prophecies and miracles can lead our friends to Jesus; but still that is no guarantee that they'll see Him for who He is.

BORN ALOFT

The Gospel itself provides us a good illustration. Consider Nicodemus, "a man of the Pharisees" and "ruler of the Jews," who "came to Jesus by night" (Jn 3:1–2). Nicodemus was certainly a theist, and beyond that a monotheist, and even further he was a devout leader of God's chosen people. He accepted God's revelation in the Old Testament. And to Jesus he made a startling admission: "Rabbi, we know that You are a teacher come from God; for no one can do these signs that you do, unless God is with him" (v. 2).

At face value, this seems to be a confession of faith. But it's not, really. Nicodemus had seen ample evidence that Jesus possessed extraordinary, supernatural power. He referred to Jesus' "signs" —His miracles. Indeed, Nicodemus was not alone in judging Jesus by His miracles. Just a few verses earlier, John had told us a curious thing: "*many* believed in His name when they saw the signs which He did; but Jesus did not trust Himself to them" (Jn 2:23–24).

It was not an act of faith for Jesus' contemporaries to hail Him as "a teacher come from God." It was a reasonable conclusion, based on hard evidence. He had changed water into wine. He had performed many wonders that His countrymen could associate with the prophets. His miracles were objects of reason, apparent to the senses. Having witnessed these wonders, the human reason could proceed by an inductive and probable path to conclude that Jesus possessed power from God.

But faith would require more. And more would require faith. For Jesus was not merely a teacher or a prophet. He was the Son of God, the eternal Word become flesh.

Jesus responded to Nicodemus's testimony by pointing out the limitations of his friend's spiritual vision: "Truly, truly, I say to you, unless one is born anew, he cannot see the kingdom of God" (Jn 3:3). Nicodemus had come to Jesus "by night" in more senses than one. He was dwelling in darkness, which could not be overcome except by the new birth of baptism.

Still, Nicodemus did not believe. Jesus' words seemed bizarre to him, as he judged them only in natural terms: "How can a man be born when he is old? Can he enter a second time into his mother's womb and be born?" (Jn 3:4). Yet Jesus insisted, and still Nicodemus persisted in his incredulity.

Finally, Jesus declared: "I say to you, we speak of what we know, and bear witness to what we have seen; but you do not receive our testimony. If I have told you earthly things and you do not believe, how can you believe if I tell you heavenly things?" (Jn 3:11–12). The scene concludes with Jesus revealing Himself as "He who descended from heaven, the Son of Man" (3:13), whose mission is to share "eternal life" with "whoever believes in Him" (Jn 3:15).

Nicodemus—and apparently many others—were willing to accept Jesus as an extraordinary man, and even as God's messenger, but not (yet) as God. And that is precisely the movement that would have carried them beyond the limits of reason and into the realm of faith. I'm not saying that it would be an unreasonable or absurd "leap into darkness" for them. In fact, I believe the opposite is true. It is reasonable to trust the message of a messenger who has established His credibility. Jesus did the things that prophets do, and He did them to a far-surpassing degree. He had given His contemporaries strong motives for trusting Him—strong reasons to believe. Still, the decision to believe would remain with them, as it remains today with all people endowed with free will.

To recognize the divine messenger is an act of natural *belief*—based on human *reason*. To see the eternal Son of God requires nothing less than supernatural *faith*—based on divine *grace*. The latter act builds on the former.

THE PROPHET MOTIVE

Nicodemus mentions "signs," but surely He also recognized the pattern of prophecy in the life of Jesus Christ. We, too, should recognize it, and we should help others see it in turn.

One of early Christianity's most persuasive arguments was the "proof from prophecy." The Church Fathers and apologists demonstrated in great detail how Jesus corresponded to the Messiah foretold by Israel's prophets. The Old Testament served as a fixed and objective rule by which anyone could measure the truth about Jesus' person and mission. These apologetic arguments fill volumes of the second-century Fathers Justin, Melito, and Irenaeus, but here is just a sampling of the hundreds of correspondences they note:

- The Messiah would be born a child, but would be "mighty God" (Is 9:6–7).
- He would be born of a virgin (Is 7:14).
- He would be born in Bethlehem (Mic 5:2).
- He would be born into the line of King David (Jer 23:5).
- He would heal the blind, lame, and deaf (Is 35:5–6).
- He would be betrayed by a friend (Ps 55:12–14).
- He would suffer and be despised (Is 53:2–7).
- His flock would abandon Him (Zech 13:7).
- He would be "pierced" by nails and by a sword (Ps 22:16, Zech 12:10).
- He would be a "just man" tortured and killed by His enemies (Wis 2:12–20).
- He would be executed with criminals (Is 53:12).
- His enemies tore His garments and gambled for them (Ps 22:18).
- He would rise from the dead (Ps 16:10, 30:3).
- He would bring all the nations the light of the true God (Is 60:3).

Again, the list goes on to fill volumes. In Jesus' life, all these prophecies coalesced and found fulfillment, in a way that boggles the human mind, but had been omnipresent in the mind of God.

Perhaps it is difficult for us, today, to understand the powerful and cumulative effect of the prophetic argument. We do not esteem prophets as our ancestors did. But the "proof from prophecy" was, for the first Christians, an appeal to the historical record. The events of Jesus' life were attested by eyewitnesses; and the books of the prophets had been a matter of public record for many centuries. Judging by the paper trail of the Church Fathers, the "proof from prophecy" must have been Christianity's most effective argument addressed to the ancient world. It is the undercurrent in the entire Acts of the Apostles. And it seems to have been as persuasive to Greeks as to Jews, since Irenaeus (for example) was writing for the benefit of second-century gentiles.

The proof from prophecy offers powerful reasons to believe, powerful *motives of credibility*. Like miracles, prophecies can bring us to the very threshold of supernatural faith, demonstrating God's guiding hand in history as He anticipated future events and confirmed past predictions. They do not, however, provide us with a rational demonstration for the supernatural mystery of faith—nor do they possess the persuasive power to bring us all the way home. Faith remains a God-given grace that requires our trusting response—to our divine Father, not merely our Creator.

In sum, our reasoning has very real, but limited, powers. It can clear the ground, by removing the stumps and stones, but only faith can construct the cathedral.

Sign Language

The miracles recounted in the first three Gospels are treated as "signs" in the fourth Gospel. For St. John the Evangelist, a miracle is a powerful proof of Jesus' power, but it has a still greater purpose. Jesus works these visible, material, historical "signs" in order to signify something greater, invisible, spiritual, and transcendent. The transubstantiation of water into wine is a miracle that signifies the greater marvel of the Holy Eucharist. The water of baptism is a sign of a new birth into divine life. But, for our human eyes, these divine mysteries are veiled.

In speaking to Nicodemus, Jesus made it clear that baptism—the sign whose very nature I struggled with so many years ago—is the sign that gives us light to "see the kingdom of heaven." Even more, it gives us a new birth, a new family, a new home. Baptism gives us the grace to see the mysteries of Christianity through eyes of faith.

The *grace* of faith unveils the mysteries for us. In our *response* of faith, we see. And it is this sight that enables us to understand, explain, and defend the faith.

The prophets predicted that God's grace should go far beyond the promised land and the chosen people, to all the world, all the nations, all the gentiles. God, in His goodness, has made us to be the channels of that grace. When we meet theists who have not accepted Christ, we must give them reasons to believe. We must *be* good reasons to believe—like the prophets and like Jesus, whose life we share.

II

Biblical Reasons

Six

BIBLE STEADY

On the Church as One Foundation

So far we have kept our focus, for the most part, on our conversations with non-Christians—whether theist or atheist, agnostic or secularist. It is a variegated category, but a useful one nonetheless, since all of its inhabitants share one thing in common: they profess unbelief, or at least neutrality, on the identity of Jesus Christ.

It is a different matter when we speak with non-Catholic Christians, especially those who hold to the traditions arising from the Protestant Reformation. In these conversations, we have much more common language, common cause, and common ground for discussion. We can assume in almost all Christians a firm belief in God, a reverence for Jesus Christ, a sense that the world is tainted by sin, and a conviction that Jesus has somehow saved us from that sin. We also hold in common our faith in the Bible as a divinely inspired, authoritative text. According to Catholic doctrine, all non-Catholic Christians share with us—though imperfectly—the one faith of Jesus Christ.

We have closer degrees of kinship with separated Christians. Once again, that can make conversation easier in some respects, but more difficult in others. We have fewer differences with other Christians than we have with non-Christians, but our differences involve key areas of belief and devotion, and so they involve matters about which all sides are passionate. Our differences are more like domestic disputes, and any policeman can tell you that those calls can be the most dangerous of all. Sibling rivalry has the potential to fuel much more hatred than even the most intense competitions between sports teams.

Thus, our conversations with other Christians can indeed be the most difficult of all. Sometimes our differences turn on slight shades of meaning that are perceived clearly only by sages and scholars. Yet Christians who have little understanding will reduce them to slogans and rush with them into battle, flush with adrenaline but ill prepared for any true engagement. In such cases, tempers tend to rise while believers argue past one another, using the same words to mean opposite realities and, in any event, each not listening to what the other person is saying.

The cartoonist Charles M. Schulz, creator of the "Peanuts" comic strip, put the matter in lighter terms. In one panel, he shows two young men holding slips of paper. The caption reads: "You've given me one of your tracts, sir, and I've given you one of mine . . . Now, where do we stand?" In another cartoon, a boy lies on the floor paging through the Bible while his sister looks on. He tells her: "Don't bother me . . . I'm looking for a verse of Scripture to back up one of my preconceived notions."

As we talk to other Christians about the reasons we're Catholic, we'll sometimes find ourselves (or our conversation partners) slipping into one of the roles of those cartoon figures. It's difficult not to do so! But it's a little easier to move beyond the comic if we understand what our differences are all about, and why we sometimes use the same terms to mean such vastly different things.

We should not be surprised that the sacred text presents some difficulties, conundrums, and mysteries. God is the author of the book of Scripture *and* the book of nature, and both books sometimes vex their would-be interpreters. If physicists and chemists cannot come to agreement on the meaning of their data, we should not be surprised to find believers disagreeing on the so-called "plain sense" of the Bible.

In this chapter, as in the preceding chapters, I will provide some remedial summaries of our reasons to believe in the Catholic faith. Here, as in the previous chapters, I do not pretend to provide an exhaustive study of the matter, just an introduction to the issues and some types of Catholic response. There are apologetical and doctrinal works that treat each of these subjects in great depth, and I urge you to study those as the need arises.

You Have the Rite to Remain Repentant

All Christians revere the Bible and consider it to be an authoritative text. The Catholic Church teaches that the Bible is the inspired Word of God and, as such, it is free from error. Many Protestants who differ with us about the way we interpret Scripture can at least agree with us on those basic principles. It helps if we can establish that fact from the start.

The first point where we differ is usually the place of Scripture in the structures of authority. Indeed, classic Protestantism asserts that "Scripture alone" (*sola scriptura*) is the authority for the Christian, and that the individual believer is competent, with the help of the Holy Spirit, to interpret the meaning of the Bible. Catholics, on the other hand, hold that the New Testament established certain institutions to guide us in the interpretation of Scripture, and they are *Tradition* and the *Church*.

Catholics freely acknowledge that they live within an interpretive community, and that they hold themselves accountable to that community. We measure our interpretations against those of saints and sages down through the millennia. We measure our interpretations against those of Christ's magisterium.

In practice, Protestants, too, operate within an interpretive community. Most of what they'll cite as the "plain sense" of a particular passage is actually dependent on a tradition of interpretation that they inherited within their denomination. And what is "plain" to their community is rejected by other Protestant bodies.

Within Protestant communities, too, traditions arise unnoticed and are taken for granted. Indeed, they can become integral and even central parts of a congregation's life. Everyone assumes that the practices are biblical—and indeed they arose within a certain environment of biblical interpretation—but they are no less "extra-biblical" or "merely traditional" than Catholic customs.

An Evangelical friend of mine once set out to criticize the Mass, and a conversation followed. It went like this.

"You know," he said, "I've been to your worship, and there's a lot that I liked about it. But there's one thing I found it lacked."

"What's that?"

"There's no place in your worship for someone to say, 'I accept Jesus Christ into my heart as my personal Lord and Savior.' "

"Where is that in the Bible?"

My friend was taken aback. "What?"

"Where is that in the Bible?"

My friend thought for a moment before acknowledging that it wasn't in the Bible, though he'd always assumed it was.

That Evangelical custom is a ritual, a "liturgy," kind of like the

Catholic Mass. It is part of the now-sizable body of Evangelical traditions—along with "altar calls" and the "Sinner's Prayer." Even though it isn't "biblical," strictly speaking, Catholics can acknowledge it as a beautiful rite.

But we can do more than that. We can show that Catholic worship does indeed have a place where believers accept Jesus into their hearts as their personal Lord and Savior. When the priest lifts up the host and says, "This is the Lamb of God who takes away the sins of the world," the entire congregation confesses, in words from Scripture (see Mt 8:8), "Lord, I am not worthy to receive You, but only say the word and I shall be healed." And then we go forward to receive Jesus into our hearts—His body, blood, soul, and divinity.

My point here is that it can sometimes be helpful for us to illuminate the obvious, very gently. We can stand with our Protestant friends in affirming a very high view of the Bible's authority. But we may also demonstrate that the Bible is not self-interpreting or self-authenticating. It does not yield a single plain sense to every well-intentioned interpreter. And everywhere, inevitably, it draws together interpretive communities. These communities build up their own traditions, rituals, and structures of authority—even as they assume they're going on "Scripture alone."

If we do this well, we can establish a larger patch of common ground for our subsequent discussion. We can proceed in at least qualified agreement on several key points: that Scripture is authoritative; that some forms of tradition and interpretive community are inevitable and perhaps even necessary; and that worship naturally tends to settle into ritual.

The question, then, is whether God wills a *particular* community, a *particular* tradition, and a *particular* liturgy. We Catholics believe that He does, and we have our reasons. Our challenge is to demonstrate for "Bible Christians" that our reasons are deeply biblical.

TEXT MESSAGING

Talking about our biblical reasons might require a little bit of adjustment on our part. Like Protestants, Catholics have a deep reverence for the authority of the Bible. We have some significant differences, however, in our approaches to Scripture. Sometimes, when Protestants and Catholics talk about the Bible, it can seem as if they're talking about two different books—and talking in two different languages.

We should acknowledge these differences from the start and do what we can to accommodate our friends in dialogue—without, of course, ever compromising our Catholic faith.

One major difficulty is that many Catholics have a strong aversion to a common Evangelical method of biblical application. It's called "proof-texting," and it involves the invocation of specific Bible verses as authorities for individual doctrines. Used at its worst, this method can involve wrenching texts out of context and using them in ways their original authors had never intended. One of my Protestant seminary professors used to condemn this practice with the line: "When you take a text out of context for use as a proof-text, that's a pretext." And it is that kind of abuse that has provoked in Catholics, perhaps, an extreme overreaction against the method.

But I would like to propose that we show respect for our Evangelical and classical Protestant friends by learning to "speak their language." Whenever we can (which is just about always), we should give them the Bible verses that justify our Catholic doctrines and practices.

Granted, this is not what most of us do, in parish Catechism or adult-education class. But it is what many Protestants do, and we should respect their methods and respond to them in a way they will understand.

In doing so, we're following the example of Jesus, who witnessed in many different ways. Sometimes He just looked at someone and said, "Come and see" (Jn 1:46). But for those who wanted proofs from Scripture, He provided proofs from Scripture: "Jesus answered them, 'You are wrong, because you know neither the scriptures nor the power of God . . . And as for the resurrection of the dead, have you not read what was said to you by God, 'I am the God of Abraham, and the God of Isaac, and the God of Jacob'? He is not God of the dead, but of the living" (Mt 22:29–32, citing Ex 3:6; see also Jn 10:34).

The weakness of proof-texting is that it can seem to pit one passage of Scripture against another passage of Scripture that seems to contradict it. And when this happens, which side wins out—the one with the largest pile of proof-texts? Unfortunately, that doesn't always work as an accurate measurement, since it might only indicate a more expensive package of Bible-search software!

And there are ample opportunities for such conflict. Medieval Christians considered the resolution of these difficulties an important part of higher education. They called such exercises *Sic et Non*—"Yes and No."

So I acknowledge the difficulties in this approach. And I heartily agree that often the "Come and see" approach is the most suitable and effective. Yet there are other times when it is simply more courteous for us to try to meet other Christians in the way they feel most comfortable. (If we follow the program I'm outlining in this book, we should arrive at a genuinely Catholic way to be immersed in the Bible—which will help us be more comfortable in those conversations, too.)

At its best, the common evangelical practice of citation shows an

admirable use of memorization—a valuable tool of learning that
has been too often neglected in recent generations. In Jesus' day,
however—and down through Middle Ages, and indeed till the mid-
twentieth century—memorization laid solid foundations for an individual's future learning. I know of some evangelical churches that
require new members to undergo a course of memorizing hundreds
of key Scripture verses. To modern Catholics, this might seem unusual. But it's not very different from our old practice of memorizing the *Baltimore Catechism* or the *Penny Catechism*, which Catholic
grade-school students ordinarily had to do before receiving Confirmation. The Evangelical courses often organize their verses themat-
ically or situationally, much as the old catechisms arranged their
doctrinal questions. Thus, both Catholics and Protestants have
used similar methods for storing doctrines up for future retrieval.

Memorization has its place, and we would do well to imitate
some non-Catholic Christians, at least in their eagerness to assim-
ilate the Word of God.

In true dialogue, it is considered impolite to insist always on our
own way of speaking. We may think as we wish, but we should
speak so as to be understood.

Jump back a few chapters for a moment. Why did we exclusively
use the language of reason and experience when preparing to witness to atheists? Why not let loose a storm of Scripture quotes?
Quite simply because atheists and agnostics do not accept the authority of the Bible. So such testimony would likely be fruitless.
With nonbelievers we do better to use the common language of
common sense. With non-Catholic Christians, however, Scripture
itself can provide a common language and common ground for
meeting one another.

We should not, moreover, be afraid to affirm a high view of the
historical value of the Bible—both the New Testament and the

Old Testament. Though only the debunkers seem to make the news, much of modern archaeology and textual scholarship has actually upheld the Scriptures' testimony, and especially the Catholic interpretation. I can mention only a few authors here, but they are representative of many more. Kenneth Kitchen's book *On the Reliability of the Old Testament* should satisfy critics who are familiar with the state of academic research. Kitchen shows solid historical grounds for many crucial (and often contested) details of the biblical record, such as the Ark of the Covenant, the name of Abraham, and even the date at which humans began to domesticate camels! The agnostic historian William Dever has written many popular treatments of the same material. N. T. Wright is a profound and prolific expositor of the historical content of the New Testament.

To *believe* the Bible—along with *believing in* the Bible—is not just for Evangelicals. A growing body of evidence indicates that it's the most reasonable reading of the historical record.

The bottom line is this: we don't need to apologize for citing chapter and verse in our apologetics. Still, in this chapter and the next two chapters, I would like to trace the lines of some fuller biblical arguments for the Catholic faith.

WHICH CAME FIRST?

We must begin from the Bible, because the New Testament is indisputably the most complete and reliable historical record of first-generation Christianity. It is our fail-safe starting point. We can fortify our biblical witness with the interpretations and confirmations of the generations immediately after the apostolic era, but we always return to the Bible—which always leads us in turn to the Church.

For the Bible does not create the Church or justify the Church or serve as the Church's constitution. The Bible presupposes the Church and depends upon the Church for its own authentication.

Once said, it seems self-evident, but it bears repeating: *The Bible presupposes the Church*. The New Testament was not a user's manual for a Church still in shrinkwrap. The Church preceded the Scriptures. Indeed, all of the New Testament books, except the Gospels, are primarily occupied with describing a community already well established, with distinctive policies, practices, and patterns of devotion—with its own structures of authority and methods of decision making. The Acts of the Apostles recounts the establishment of the Church in the towns and cities visited by the apostles. The letters of Paul, Peter, John, James, and Jude address the general concerns and questions of those scattered assemblies, once established by the apostles. The Book of Revelation looks at those earthly congregations from a heavenly vantage point, now that they have matured and even had time to stray from the normative ways laid down by the apostles. Again, all of this presumes a widespread Church, long established, with identifiable doctrine and practice.

Here we should note that Jesus Himself wrote nothing and, as far as we know, He never asked His disciples to write anything. His significant command to them was "do this," not "write this"; and "this" referred to the Church-forming sacrament of His body and blood.

But there is still another sense in which the Bible depends upon the Church. Not only do the individual books presume the existence of the Church, but so does the collection as a whole. Some authority had to determine which books would be included in the New Testament and which would not; for the book of the Scriptures came with no inspired table of contents. There were, moreover, many contenders for sacred status—letters, "gospels," and "revelations" attributed to various apostles—and some of these were even considered "scriptural" in different congregations.

It was not until the fourth and fifth centuries that the institutional Church fixed the New Testament in the form we know it today; and it was brought to that form, after a thorough investigation, through the work of bishops and synods of bishops—a process familiar to Catholics of every historical age since the first generation. The complete Christian "canon," or list of New Testament Scriptures, was attested by St. Athanasius in 367 A.D., but accepted universally only with the Synod of Rome in 380 and the Councils of Hippo and Carthage (in 393, 397, and 417 A.D.). The pseudonymous books, sometimes called "New Testament apocrypha," had long since been discredited, so there was no debate about their inclusion. But *exclusion* was quite another matter. Up until the last minute, misguided scholars argued for the removal of the books of Revelation, Hebrews, Second Peter, and others. The settlement of the canon was certainly God's will, but it was not a foregone conclusion, by any human measure.

Through all those centuries, the biblical books existed, though they did not exist as a clearly defined collection. Yet they were protected, proclaimed, and passed down by the very Church from which they had first emerged. The Church that canonized the Scriptures was the very Church that had produced them, though in a generation long past.

Since the Protestant Reformation, many people have tried to build the Church anew based on the evidence they find in the New Testament. But they cannot agree on what exactly the New Testament means when it describes a Church, and how such a Church would look two thousand years down the line. The wiser course is to look to the Church that came before the Scriptures—the

Church that produced the Scriptures with divine assistance, and that preserved their integrity through the threats of persecution and heresy—the Church that gathered the Scriptures together in a book—a book that sustains all who call themselves Christians today.

ON YOUR MARKS

In any discussion about the Church, a Catholic should have an advantage in beginning from the Bible, because the New Testament authors took great pains to describe a Church that would be exemplary and normative for all subsequent generations—and that Church looks a lot like our own. Let's illustrate the similarities with just a few distinctive examples, which are (again) indicative of many other instances.

How can we recognize the true Church of Jesus Christ? In the fourth century, the Fathers of the Church looked at the biblical testimony and discerned four strong characteristics of the Church: it is one, holy, catholic, and apostolic.

The Church is One.

St. Paul emphasized that, just as there is one Lord and one God, so there is "one faith, one baptism" (Eph 4:5). Repeatedly, he described the Church as "one body," identified with the integrity and uniqueness of Jesus' own body (Rom 12:5; I Cor 10:17, 12:12–13; Eph 2:16, 4:4; Col 3:15). Paul acknowledges that Christians are many and diverse, but he insists on the Church's unity, and he casts that unity in sacramental terms: "For by one Spirit we were all baptized into one body . . . and all were made to drink of one Spirit" (I Cor 12:13). Christians are bound together by common baptism and the Eucharist. God has endowed the Church with such mighty graces that even angels see God's plan unfold through the Church (Eph 3:10).

Some people object that this "Church" is a purely spiritual or merely figurative reality. But that is not what Paul seems to mean when he speaks of the Church as the "body" of Christ. For a body is the visible part of a being endowed with a soul. If Paul had wanted to describe a purely spiritual Church, he could have called it the "soul" of Christ, but "body" would be an unlikely choice—especially for a metaphor so dominant in his writing.

If "body" has any meaning whatsoever as a metaphor, it must indicate a visible unity. Jesus Himself expressed a profound desire for Church unity. Evoking many Old Testament texts, He promised, "There shall be one flock, one shepherd" (Jn 10:16).

We can be sure that neither Jesus nor St. Paul intended a vague unity that glossed over difference. On the contrary, Paul says, "I appeal to you, brethren, by the name of our Lord Jesus Christ, that all of you agree and that there be no dissensions among you, but that you be united in the same mind and the same judgment" (I Cor 1:10).

The only candidate for such unity is the Catholic Church, which transcends all ethnic, national, and cultural boundaries. It is the only Christian body that professes one faith, undivided, unchanged, throughout the world and throughout the ages. Those separated Christians who profess "scripture alone," on the other hand, have multiplied denominations into the tens of thousands. And those Christian *bodies* differ from one another on such key matters as the nature of the atonement and the meaning of charismatic gifts, the appropriate age for baptism and the optimum frequency of communion, the morality of abortion and euthanasia, the nature and function of the clergy, even the day of the week on which Christians should worship. Many of these interpretations are mutually contradictory and mutually exclusive. Denominations as large as the Lutherans and the Baptists disagree profoundly on the nature of the sacraments. Could such confusion be what Jesus and St. Paul meant by the Church's unity?

Compare these many denominations with the Church of the New Testament—the united Church in which "churches" are divided geographically, but never along denominational or doctrinal lines. That sort of diversity is rejected. The only alternative Christian group we encounter is the Nicolaitans, who are deplored precisely because of their doctrinal aberrations (Rev 2:15).

Outside the Catholic Church, there are many voices competing, all claiming the Bible as their basis. In the Catholic Church, however, we have one voice, the voice of Christ down through the ages.

The Church is unified through two millennia and throughout every inhabited continent. The snapshot of the Church taken in the Acts of the Apostles really could have been taken at any point in the Church's history, and anywhere on God's earth: "And they devoted themselves to the apostles' teaching and fellowship, to the breaking of bread and the prayers" (Acts 2:42). Wherever the Catholic Church goes, the people assemble to hear the apostolic doctrine and commune in the broken bread, saying the accustomed prayers.

This is not to say that the Catholic Church has no grumblers in its pews, no rebels, no dissenters, or no sinners. But the Church remains one despite the sort of characters we meet in those same pages of the Acts of the Apostles—characters like Ananias and Sapphira (Acts 5:1–11), Simon Magus of Samaria (Acts 8:9–24), and their ilk. Think, too, of the reprobates Paul mentions in his First Letter to the Corinthians.

The Church is divine, but it is also human. This is the mystery of its embodied life. When God became incarnate, His crucified body was covered with grime and spittle. In every age, the sinners within the Church (and we are all sinners) are the grime on the Body of Christ.

In the Catholic experience, even the sinners witness to the oneness of the Church! The novelist James Joyce rather famously nicknamed the Catholic Church "HCE" for "Here Comes Everybody."

The word "mystery" is important here, because it is yet another word that St. Paul applies to the Church (Eph 5:32). A mystery is something hidden from sight, something that can be known by faith alone. When we look at the Church, we see and hear its human element, a sociological phenomenon. But, with eyes of faith, we, like Paul, must discern a true mystery, the one and only "body of Christ." That means affirming something that is not apparent to the eyes. It is a matter of supernatural faith.

The Church is Holy.

The New Testament speaks often of the Church in terms of holiness. The Church is a "holy nation" (1 Pet 2:9). It is the Bride of Christ (Eph 5:31–32). It is the "temple of the living God" (2 Cor 6:16). As we mentioned before, the Church is the holy Body of Christ.

The Church's members are "holy ones" (Acts 9:13; 1 Cor 6:1), or "saints," depending on the translation of Scripture you use.

The concept of holiness is central to biblical religion, in both the Old Testament and the New Testament. The prophet Daniel foresees that "saints of the Most High shall receive the kingdom, and possess the kingdom for ever, for ever and ever" (Dn 7:18).

The Hebrew word for holiness is *kiddushin*. Literally, it means "set apart"—reserved for a special purpose—as the Temple is set apart from other buildings, as the Sabbath is set apart from other days, and as a bride is "set apart" for her groom. (In fact, *kiddushin* can also mean "wedding.") God's holy people are those He has set aside from all the rest of creation, to be the crown of His creation, His greatest glory in creation—not merely His creatures or His servants (which would be honor enough), but His beloved sons and daughters.

The Church is holy because it shares His divine life. As the Body of Christ, the Church possesses and dispenses the very life of Christ. Its members are holy because, by baptism, they are "partakers of the divine nature" (2 Pet 1:4). That's the meaning of grace: a share of God's own life.

The people the Church honors as "saints" are those who corresponded in an exemplary way with God's grace. Often this grace manifested itself in outward signs, such as a heroically virtuous life, a martyr's death, or even the working of great miracles.

Yet we must be careful here. Many people today equate holiness with mere righteousness or good behavior, but they're not the same thing—though the two qualities must coexist in the same soul. (That is the literal meaning of "justification" and "sanctification." We are "made righteous" and "made holy.") Holiness is the divine life, the life of Christ reproduced in the life and death of the saint. In the martyr this is reproduced in a vivid and pre-eminent way. And it is this Christ-life that sparks our reverence and awe.

The ancient Church venerated the martyrs. We see that in the New Testament (Heb 11:35–38, Rev 6:9–11). But the earliest Christians venerated another group even more than the martyrs. In time, some authors would say that this other group lived a kind of "white martyrdom," dying not in a blaze of glorious violence, but dying to self, quietly, over the ordinary course of a lifetime. This group comprised those Christians who had renounced normal family life for the sake of Christ and His kingdom. They were the Church's celibate members and consecrated virgins.

Jesus praises celibates as those "who have made themselves eunuchs for the sake of the kingdom of heaven" (Mt 19:12). In the ancient world, eunuchs were castrated men in the royal court, many of whom were charged with guarding the king's harem (see, for example, Acts 8:27f). They were incapable of sexual relations, and so could be trusted to attend to matters of state, without the distractions or temptations that might beset the king's other ministers. But Jesus is not speaking about physical eunuchs. He is explaining that, in the New Covenant, there will be celibate men who renounce sex and marriage so that they can guard the Church, the true bride of the King of Kings. Jesus concludes that such an office is not for everyone, but that "He who is able to receive this, let him receive it" (Mt 19:12).

St. Paul devotes the greater part of a chapter in his First Letter to the Corinthians to the care of virgins (chapter 7). While Paul affirms the good of marriage, he returns repeatedly to the superiority of celibacy (vv. 1, 7, 8, 27–35, 38, 40), citing his own personal experience. The Book of Revelation presents virgins and celibates as those who are already living as if they are in heaven, unencumbered as they follow Christ: "for they are chaste; it is these who follow the Lamb wherever he goes; these have been redeemed from mankind as first fruits for God and the Lamb" (Rev 14:4). Indeed, Jesus Himself emphasized celibacy as a condition of heavenly life (see Mk 12:25), and Paul spoke of consecrated virgins as "those who deal with the world as though they had no dealings with it. For the form of this world is passing away" (1 Cor 7:31).

Throughout the first centuries of Christianity, the Church continued to observe and revere virginity and celibacy, often invoking the New Testament precedents. An early Christian apologist named

St. Aphrahat noted, moreover, that celibacy is not merely a blessing of the New Testament, but also of the Old. He pointed out that temporary abstinence was a condition of Moses' sanctification of Israel (Ex 19:10, 15), and that Joshua, Jeremiah, Elijah, and Elisha were celibate—Jeremiah by the explicit command of the Lord (Jer 16:2). And it was customary, too, for Israel's priests to refrain from having normal marital relations during their service in the sanctuary.

None of this implies that marriage and sex are evil or somehow "dirty." Celibacy is holy precisely because of the value of what is sacrificed. No one would attempt to consecrate garbage by putting it on the altar. Marriage and sex are indeed very good gifts from our very good God. But Christians—and even the pre-Christian prophets and priests—were willing to give up something good for the sake of Someone better. They were willing to set themselves apart—which, again, is the very definition of holiness—as a sign of the holiness, the *kiddushin*, the wedding of God and His bride, the Church.

This sign of holiness is prominent in the Scriptures. It was everywhere in the ancient Church, and the medieval Church, and the Church of every subsequent age. Today, I can think of only one Christian Church where this sign of holiness is so prominent, and that is the Roman Catholic Church. Celibacy is not the sum of holiness, but it is an important sign—and a biblical sign. And all the other signs—righteousness, miracles, fidelity—attend it in abundance.

The Church is Catholic.

Many people today understand the word "catholic" to be a denominational term, like Presbyterian or Baptist. But, in fact, it is the opposite of denominational. Catholic means "universal," and that universality is a quality of the Church that was willed by Jesus Himself, when He said: "All authority in heaven and on earth has been given to Me. Go therefore and make disciples of *all nations,* baptizing them in the name of the Father and of the Son and of the Holy Spirit, teaching them to observe all that I have commanded you; and lo, I am with you *always,* to the close of the age" (Mt 28:18–20). Such catholicity came as fulfillment of many Old Testament prophecies: "all peoples, nations, and languages serve Him. His dominion is an everlasting dominion" (Dn 7:14).

Jesus conferred on the Church an authority that was properly His own, and so it extended to every place and through all time. It would be always and everywhere. The Church is not a phenomenon isolated in a geographic region, or a particular age. It belongs to no political party or ruling dynasty. It belongs to no language or language group, as the Holy Spirit so amply demonstrated on the first Pentecost with the gift of tongues (see Acts 2:4–11).

And yet there is nothing vague or indistinct about the Church's unity. The Body of Christ is recognizable in its particulars—the fellowship, the teaching of the apostles, the breaking of the bread, and the prayers (Acts 2:42). That's how it always looks, no matter where it goes.

From the beginning, Christians used the Greek word *katholikos* to describe the Church of Jesus Christ. It is derived from *kata hole,* meaning "pertaining to the whole" or, simply, "universal." The earliest literary records apart from the Bible attest to this. In 105 A.D., Ignatius of Antioch wrote to the Christians of Smyrna, "Wherever the bishop appears, let the congregation be there also, just as wherever Jesus Christ is, there is the Catholic Church." A few years later, the word appears in the account of the martyrdom of St. Ignatius's close friend, St. Polycarp, a document addressed to "the holy and catholic Church in every place." These testimonies come with a certain apostolic pedigree. Ignatius may have been a disciple of the Apostle John, and Polycarp certainly was.

Catholic doctrine and worship display remarkable unity throughout the world and throughout history. It is not mere uniformity, because styles and expressions change according to local language and custom. But still the local churches are clearly identified with the universal body. The early Christians took great pleasure in noting that that passage from Acts—about the breaking of the bread and the prayers—was no longer a snapshot of the Jerusalem Church, but a template for the universal (that is, Catholic) Church. Around the year 150, St. Justin noted that "there is not one single race of men . . . among whom prayers and Eucharist are not offered through the name of the crucified Jesus." That's ubiquity. That's catholicity. And its distinguishing mark is the breaking of the bread, that is, the Mass.

The ancient Fathers commonly applied the Old Testament prophecy of Malachi to the Mass: "from the rising of the sun to its setting my name is great among the nations, and in every place incense is offered to my name, and a pure offering" (Mal 1:11). That line appears in the earliest Eucharistic prayers we know, including the one in a document called the *Didache*, whose ritual portions probably date back to 48 A.D. The Mass was *everywhere*—even that early in history—because the Church was understood to be Catholic.

Now, some people today object that "Roman Catholic" is a contradiction in terms, because "catholic" pertains to the whole world, while Rome is just one city. But the universal Church looks to Rome because that is the city where the prince of the Apostles, Peter, ruled and died. And, when he died, the Church fulfilled the mandate of Acts 1:20: "For it is written . . . 'His office let another take.' " Peter was succeeded in his primacy by others, one of them a man named Clement, who witnessed to Rome's very catholic authority already in the mid-first century! St. Clement wrote—probably as early as 69 A.D., but certainly no later than 96—to discipline a distant congregation in Corinth. As he concluded his remonstration, he said: "You will give us joy and gladness if you render obedience to the things written by us through the Holy Spirit." So the Church of Rome, and specifically one man named Clement, spoke on earth with the authority of the Holy Spirit, and that authority extended to Christians the world over.

The Fathers of the Church amply testify to Rome's primacy. Around 105, St. Ignatius of Antioch addressed the Roman Church as "the Church worthy of God, worthy of honor, worthy of felic-itation, worthy of praise, worthy of success, worthy of sanctifica-tion, and presiding in love, maintaining the law of Christ." That is a good summary of the role that Rome has continued to fulfill in the Church in every age, "presiding in love." A few years later, in 190 A.D., St. Irenaeus—an Asian bishop serving in what is today France—paid tribute to Rome in the most deferential terms: "with this Church it is necessary that every Church, that is, the faithful who are everywhere, should be in agreement, because of her greater sovereignty; in which the apostolic tradition has always been safe-guarded." Again, from a very early date, the universal Church—those who are everywhere—looked to Rome for leadership and sure doctrine. In the following centuries, we see that the great names of Christianity—St. Athanasius, St. John Chrysostom, St. Basil of Caesarea, St. Augustine, St. Cyril of Alexandria—when they found themselves in trouble, appealed to Rome for vindica-tion.

For all these men—scattered as widely as the lands that are now called France and Turkey and Egypt—Rome was a fixed point of unity that secured the Church universal.

This unity is personified in the person of the pope, the successor of St. Peter, and that subject will be discussed more fully below (and in a later chapter of this book).

The Church is Apostolic.

As we look at this fourth and last "mark of the Church," I want to emphasize that these marks are not something the Church Fathers imagined or invented. Rather, they are the distinguishing marks the early Christians discerned upon careful reading of the Scriptures over the course of a prayerful lifetime. We are talking about something deeply biblical. The creeds that preserve the four marks are the Church's crystallized and crystal-clear reflections on the Bible. Thus, Christians who reject what the Fathers say are not arguing about philosophy or politics, but about biblical interpretation. They are taking issue with the interpretation of men who were much closer in time and culture to Jesus' own time and culture than we are today. They are rejecting biblical interpretations that have been confirmed by many generations and hallowed by time. Our Protestant-Catholic controversies are not so much a matter of "Scripture versus Tradition"—as some people make them out to be—but rather of one interpretation of Scripture against another.

Apostolicity is the fourth mark of the Church, and it is a quality deemed supremely important in the New Testament. St. Paul writes: "you are fellow citizens with the saints and members of the household of God, *built upon the foundation of the Apostles*" (Eph 2:19–20). St. John shows us that the Apostles are the "twelve foundations" of the walls of the heavenly Jerusalem" (Rev 21:14). The household of God, the heavenly city—that is, the Church—rests upon the sure foundation of its apostolicity.

The Church is apostolic in more than one sense: First, because it is founded on the Apostles, but also because it preserves their teaching and traditions; because it continues to be guided by those teachings and traditions; and because it has received the entire patrimony of the Apostles, through a legitimate succession.

Now, anyone who contends that pedigrees are alien to biblical faith has apparently never read the Bible. In both the Old Testament and the New Testament we meet authors who are preoccupied with genealogy. Consider Genesis 10–11. Consider Matthew 1. Consider Luke 3. And this preoccupation did not end with the coming of Jesus Christ. As we saw above, the Apostles were careful to choose successors. St. Peter's quotation of Psalm 108:8, "His office let another take," is illuminating. The word "office" here is a translation of the Greek word *episkopen* (literally, "overseer"), from which we derive the English word "bishop." In fact, in the Protestant King James Version of the Bible, the line is rendered, "his bishopric let another take." Luke is discussing here the "office" of Apostle, which the Church even then understood under the title "bishop."

A close collaborator of Saints Peter and Paul, St. Clement of Rome described how these men continued this practice in the later years of their apostolate. "Preaching everywhere in country and town, they appointed their firstfruits, when they had proved them by the Spirit, to be bishops and deacons unto them that should believe. This was no novelty; for indeed it had been written concerning bishops and deacons from very ancient times; for thus says the Scripture in a certain place, 'I will appoint their bishops in righteousness and their deacons in faith.' "

Clement also explains *why* his predecessors did this: "Our Apostles knew through our Lord Jesus Christ that there would be dissension over the bishop's office. That is why, having received complete foreknowledge, they appointed the aforesaid persons, and afterwards they provided a continuance, that if these should fall asleep, other approved men should succeed them in ministry."

And so the succession has continued, unbroken. St. Irenaeus wrote in 190 A.D. about the earlier popes as if he were writing about ancient history—and he was!—but he was careful to include each and every name as he traced the chain of succession down to his own day.

We, too, can trace it down to ours. For the Church still today passes on its apostolic authority as the first Apostles show us in the pages of the Bible: by the laying on of hands (see I Tim 5:22; 2 Tim 1:6).

And it is not merely a matter of credentials—though credentials, too, are important. It is a matter of "the gift"—the charisms, the grace—conferred through the imposition of divinely qualified hands (I Tim 4:14). The clergy so ordained became "stewards of the mysteries of God" (I Cor 4:1), with the God-given power to exercise that stewardship.

My friend Ian tells a story from the days when he was a Baptist preacher serving a small congregation in Texas. Ian zealously tried to bring the Gospel not only to the established families of his little church, but to their less-fortunate neighbors, many of whom were very poor. He was so successful that the church was enjoying record attendance. He had quite literally changed the complexion of the congregation, as people of different races began to appear.

But not everyone in the congregation was happy about that. In fact, some members began to organize, and they even broke into Ian's parsonage to serve him a warning that he might be fired.

Ian sought advice in his Baptist church's regional offices. But his colleagues there informed him that there was really no court of appeal beyond the congregation. Ian pointed out how that ran contrary to the New Testament example. The Apostles were not disciplined by their congregations, nor did they take orders from their congregations. Rather, it was they who presided in love over the Christian assemblies.

"Well, that's true, Ian," one colleague said. "But that's not the way we do things today."

"Well, is anyone following the New Testament on this?" Ian asked. "Who *is* doing things the New Testament way?"

The man laughed at the thought that crossed his mind. "I'm afraid the only folks who work that way anymore are the Roman Catholics."

Ian is now a Roman Catholic.

Apostolicity, like the other three marks, is more plainly evident in the Catholic Church than anywhere else on earth.

What does it mean, practically speaking? It means just what Jesus told the first Apostles it would mean. "It is not you who speak, but the Spirit of your Father speaking through you" (Mt 10:20). Notice: He did not tell them they would always be admirable characters. He told them the Spirit would speak through them (see Jn 20:21–22)—in spite of the weaknesses and limitations of their human condition. Then Jesus said: "He who hears you hears Me, and he who rejects you rejects Me, and he who rejects Me rejects Him who sent Me" (Lk 10:16).

REALITY CHECK

When we speak with non-Catholics about the Church, we will do well to dispel two common mistakes: one would reduce the Church to a merely sociological phenomenon—nothing more than a visible, earthly institution—while the other would spiritualize the Church beyond the possibility of any true earthly presence.

The Church is indeed a supernatural reality. Its deepest dimensions are not apparent to our senses. Like the divinity of Jesus and like the incarnation of God, the Church is a supernatural object of our faith. And faith is the only appropriate response. The Church—again like the incarnation—is not merely spiritual and certainly not just theoretical or ideal. The Church is God's visible body. God is now our Temple, our bread, our bath, and our anointing. He is present in the Word we hear proclaimed from the sanctuary. We need not fear we'll extol the Church too much, or extol the Church at the expense of Jesus Christ. The Church is Christ's work. He said, "On this rock *I* will build *My* Church" (Mt 16:18). So the more we make of the Church, the more we make of Him— and of the Holy Spirit. For it is to the Holy Spirit that we credit the Church's oneness, holiness, catholicity, and apostolicity. Once, when a non-Catholic friend challenged me on my devotion to the Church, I replied, "If Catholics are wrong about the Church's oneness, sacraments, and saints, then it's because we give the Holy Spirit too much credit! But I don't think we can or do."

The Church of Christ is solid, identifiable, and within reach of all of us. It has bulk and heft—"the church of the living God, the pillar and bulwark of the truth" (I Tim 3:15).

The Catholic Church—which produced and canonized the New Testament—is the Church revealed throughout the New Testament.

Is it possible to read another kind of Church into the pages of the Bible? It is indeed, but only if we choose to place ourselves in judgment of all the interpreters of the early Church—the men who received the apostolic succession, and were in a position to know better. This should require a tremendous amount of fear and trembling, if not for the natural reasons, then surely for the supernatural reasons. For Jesus said to His first Apostles: "He who rejects you rejects Me."

Seven

SAINTS ALIVE

On Love and the Limits of Human Fellowship

Before I was Catholic, I could, at the slightest provocation, multiply objections to Catholic beliefs and practices. But my imposing list of objections sometimes boiled down to one big concern: the fear of idolatry. I was not alone in this, and not entirely at fault. Many Protestants worry that Catholics, by their veneration of human beings, might be putting mere creatures in the place of God. After all, in the very first of the Ten Commandments, God prohibits such misdirected worship, and He does so in the most explicit terms:

> I am the Lord your God, who brought you out of the land
> of Egypt, out of the house of bondage. You shall have no
> other gods before Me. You shall not make for yourself a
> graven image, or any likeness of anything that is in heaven
> above, or that is in the earth beneath, or that is in the water
> under the earth; you shall not bow down to them or serve
> them; for I the Lord your God am a jealous God.
> (Ex 20:2–5)

The jealousy I felt on God's behalf was misguided, but I think it was also understandable and even praiseworthy. At least that's what I think when I encounter it in Protestants today.

For me, the First Commandment implied an almost absolute ban on honoring the dead. The preachers I admired most would react with horror to common Catholic ways of showing reverence for the saints in heaven: their depiction in icons and monuments; their invocation in prayers; the veneration of their relics; and so on. I believed that such homage belonged to God alone. Furthermore, I invoked the biblical injunctions against necromancy (communication with the dead) as prohibiting any active fellowship between Christians on earth and the saints in heaven.

I was wrong, but, again, my concerns arose from the noblest motivations. I wished God to be worshiped as He wills to be worshiped.

Yet that is precisely what Catholics want as well! And that is one reason I was, eventually, drawn to the Catholic Church. As I studied the matter, I learned that Catholics have strong biblical reasons to believe as they do—and to act on their belief in the ways that they have since Christ founded His Church. Let's look more closely at what the Bible has to say about the saints in heaven—and the terms of their relationship with us, the saints on earth.

Cloud Cover

The New Testament gives us several precious glimpses of the afterlife of God's faithful people, and all our doctrine and practices follow from these revelations.

The Letter to the Hebrews, especially in chapter 11, speaks of the Old Testament heroes in honorific terms: Abraham and Sarah, Isaac and Jacob, Joseph and Moses, David and Samuel, and many others make their appearance. Their lives on earth, the author says, prepared them for a greater life in a heavenly homeland. "These all died in faith, not having received what was promised, but having seen it and greeted it from afar ... Therefore God is not ashamed to be called their God, for He has prepared for them a city" (Heb 11:13, 16). Now, with Christ's redemption, the promise has been fulfilled, the heavenly city given to the faithful. They are there, says the Letter to the Hebrews, and yet they are also with us; for they surround us as "so great a cloud of witnesses" (Heb 12:1).

Why did the inspired author recall these great figures from long-ago history? I believe he had several reasons. First, he wanted to inspire his readers—who were then facing persecution—to imitate the patriarchs' virtuous example. He presents the ancestors as "witnesses," and witnesses give testimony. Israel's patriarchs continued to testify as the Church remembered their earthly deeds. The bright lights of salvation history had kept the faith, even though it had cost them everything, even as they "suffered mocking and scourging ... chains and imprisonment," even though they "were stoned ... sawn in two ... killed with the sword ... destitute, afflicted, ill-treated" (Heb 11:36–27). As Christians heard the testimony of the lives of these witnesses, they were fortified for their own trials. But witnesses do more than testify. Witnesses also observe. And the author of Hebrews wanted his readers to know that Christians were not alone in their struggles, that the bygone heroes were with them, watching from a homeland that would one day belong to *everyone* who persevered in the faith. Nor are the saints watching from a distance. They "surround" the faithful on earth.

The Old Testament saints dwell in "a cloud," we are told, an enveloping cloud. And that phrase was ripe with meaning for a first-century Jewish audience. For "the Hebrews," to whom the letter is addressed, the cloud was *God's glory*, plain and simple. When

God had guided their ancestors through the desert, He appeared to them by day as a pillar of cloud. When He was present among them in the tabernacle (and later in the Temple), they saw only His *Shekinah*, the glory cloud that attended Him. In the New Testament, the same cloud descended to lift Jesus up to heaven before the wondering eyes of His disciples. So the faithful departed who now dwelt in the "cloud of witnesses" were quite literally saints *in glory*.

Jesus is enthroned *in glory*, in that "cloud," where He is the "first-born among many brethren" (Rom 8:29). Since the day of Jesus' enthronement, the Old Testament saints enjoyed a glory they had not known before. At first they "did not receive what was promised" (Heb 11:39); but now they are in the promised homeland, even as they surround the Church in a cloud. In the Book of Revelation, we see with St. John that there are "a hundred and forty-four thousand sealed, out of every tribe of the sons of Israel" (Rev 7:4).

And if that is true for the saints of the Old Covenant, how much more for the saints of the New!

WHAT THE SEER SAW

So we know the saints are in glory. It is fair to ask, however, how they live now, and what might be the limits of their knowledge and activity. The Book of Revelation gives us answers.

John the Seer could "see" heaven because he had entered the glory cloud. When he received his vision, he was "in the Spirit on the Lord's day" (Rev 1:10). Amid the hosts of heaven, he saw a multitude of saints, but he distinguished those in three categories: martyrs, virgins, and confessors. His first encounter with the martyrs is especially telling:

I saw under the altar the souls of those who had been slain
for the word of God and for the witness they had borne;
they cried out with a loud voice, "O Sovereign Lord, holy
and true, how long before You will judge and avenge our
blood on those who dwell upon the earth?" Then they were
each given a white robe and told to rest a little longer, until
the number of their fellow servants and their brethren
should be complete, who were to be killed as they themselves
had been." (Rev 6:9–11)

So what do we know about the martyrs in heaven, based on this
brief passage? We know that they communicate with God: They
call out to Him, and He responds. We know that they are aware of
events on earth, and that they plead the cause of the just against
the unjust, the Church against its persecutors. We know, too, that
they have some foreknowledge of the future, by the grace of God.
They know how events will play out for "their fellow servants and
their brethren." What we see in Revelation confirms what we have
read in Hebrews: the martyrs in heaven are a "cloud of witnesses"
around their fellow Christians on earth. Furthermore, they are in-
tercessors in heaven for the cause of the Church on earth.

In the next chapter of Revelation, we meet the confessors, those
"who have come out of the great tribulation; they have washed
their robes and made them white in the blood of the Lamb" (Rev
7:14). We learn that this group stands "before the throne of God,
and serve Him day and night within His temple" (v. 15). Their service, of course, is prayer, as we learn a few verses later: "And another angel came and stood at the altar with a golden censer; and
he was given much incense to mingle with the prayers of all the
saints upon the golden altar before the throne; and the smoke of
the incense rose with the prayers of the saints from the hand of the

angel before God" (8:3–4). Their powerful prayer, mediated by angels, rises in heaven, but has immediate effects upon earth: "Then the angel took the censer and filled it with fire from the altar and threw it on the earth; and there were peals of thunder, voices, flashes of lightning, and an earthquake" (v. 5).

So we see again not only that the saints are in conversation with God, but also that their conversation touches upon earthly matters, and that their conversation has an immediate and powerful effect on earthly events.

The saints receive this power as a blessing from God. John reports a voice saying: "Blessed are the dead who die in the Lord henceforth." "Blessed indeed," says the Spirit, "that they may rest from their labors, for their deeds follow them!" (Rev 14:13).

It is clear from John's Revelation that the blessings of the saints in heaven cascade from them to bless the earth as well.

ONE MEDIATOR

In my own journey toward Catholicism, I eventually came to accept the notion of the saints' knowledge of earthly events, but I drew the line at their intercessory power. I would cite St. Paul's First Letter to Timothy: "For there is one God, and there is one mediator between God and men, the man Christ Jesus" (1 Tim 2:5).

In quoting that passage by itself, however, I was wrenching it out of its context. To understand it properly—and in a way that confirms Catholic teaching on intercessory prayer—I needed to back up just a few verses. Here is the passage in its entirety, from the beginning of the chapter:

> First of all, then, I urge that supplications, prayers,
> intercessions, and thanksgivings be made for all men, for

kings and all who are in high positions, that we may lead a quiet and peaceable life, godly and respectful in every way. This is good, and it is acceptable in the sight of God our Savior, who desires all men to be saved and to come to the knowledge of the truth. For there is one God, and there is one mediator between God and men, the man Christ Jesus, who gave Himself as a ransom for all.

Now, what conclusions can we draw from that? Can we really conclude that saints who intercede for one another are undermining the mediatorship of Jesus Christ? No, of course not. St. Paul is *urging* Christians to intercede for one another. He's *urging* them to act as mediators on behalf of specific groups of people: civic leaders, for example. He's emphasizing that such mediation is "acceptable in the sight of God"—and that it is efficacious: "that we may lead a quiet and peaceable life." So intercessory prayer is not only approved; it's guaranteed to make a difference.

Christ is indeed the one mediator; but the saints share His mediation because they share His life. Now, remember what the New Testament authors mean when they speak of the "saints." They mean the "holy ones," those who have been sanctified by baptism; and that includes the faithful on earth as well as in heaven. All the faithful are "in Christ," to use St. Paul's favorite phrase. Whether in heaven or on earth, the saints can intercede for others *precisely because they share the life of this one mediator and He lives in them.* Jesus said: "If you abide in Me, and My words abide in you, ask whatever you will, and it shall be done for you. By this My Father is glorified" (Jn 15:7–8). So the intercession of the saints steals nothing from God's glory. We do not glorify the saints *in place of* God, but we glorify them *in* God. He Himself has shared His glory with them, as He welcomed them into the glory cloud and made it a great "cloud of witnesses."

We can thank God that these witnesses are not mere observers or helpless bystanders. They don't just stand there. They do something. Christlike, they plead for us at the right hand of the Father. It is Christ who has given them the privilege of interceding in this way. It is Christ who invests their prayers with power, as He invests our own prayers—the intercessory prayers of the saints on earth. "We are God's co-workers" (1 Cor 3:9).

So, when we honor the saints, we are imitating Christ, who honored them first. We honor those whom He honors. We bless those whom He blesses: "Blessed are the dead who die in the Lord" (Rev 14:13).

Still, some might ask whether it is permissible for Christians to traffic with the dead, a practice forbidden in the Old Testament (see Lev 20:27, Dt 18:11). Ours is the answer evident from Hebrews and Revelation and the entire New Testament. "For me to live is Christ," said St. Paul, "and to die is gain" (Phil 1:21). The saints in heaven have entered fully into life with God, and they are more alive than we are, more alive than anyone to whom we might speak on earth. For God "is not God of the dead, but of the living" (Mk 12:27).

METAPHYSICAL GRAFFITI

Knowing well these passages from Scripture, the early Christians kept a lively devotion to the saints. The ancient pilgrimage sites are covered with graffiti etched in stone and plaster in the first centuries after Jesus' ascension. "Help me, St. Crescens!" "Peter, ask Christ Jesus!" "Peter and Paul, pray for Victor!"

The ancient Christians did not adore the saints, nor do Catholics today. The Book of Revelation makes clear that adoration belongs only to God: seeing an angel, John "fell down at his feet to worship him, but he said to me, 'You must not do that! I am a fellow servant with you and your brethren who hold the testimony of Jesus. Worship God' " (Rev 19:10). We worship God. We adore Him. We honor the saints, and we venerate them—because that's what Christ does!

Saints are not divine, except in the sense that all Christians are divinized (see 2 Pet 1:4). They deserve reverence insofar as they are vessels of God's holiness. All the saints, on earth and in heaven, share in His holiness. But only God *is* holy (see Rev 15:4). Likewise, the saints are finite; only God is infinite. The saints are creatures; but God is the creator. The saints *have* being, while God *is* Being itself. The saints would, each and all, be lost and dead in sin, were it not for the grace of Jesus Christ.

We Christians honor the saints because they are God's. We worship God because He is.

Mary, Quite Contrary

What we have said of the great cloud of saints is true, many times over, of the Blessed Virgin Mary. Still, she requires special treatment here, because those Protestants who reject Catholic doctrine on the saints tend to reject, many times over, Catholic doctrine on Mary. For me, she was a large obstacle on the way to Catholic faith.

Mary holds a unique place in the Communion of Saints. God gave her a pivotal role in history, as He became incarnate in her womb. He allowed the course of redemption to turn on her consent. He ordained that her life, interwoven as it was with the life of Jesus, should fulfill many of the foreshadowings of the Old Testament.

No one can deny that Mary bore a blessing that was singular since the beginning of the world. In Revelation, God proclaims,

"Blessed are the dead who die in the Lord." Yet Mary is blessed at the very moment we encounter her in the pages of the Gospels (see Lk 1:42).

She is, in fact, more than merely blessed. We learn from her angelic visitor, at the beginning of Luke's Gospel, that Mary is "full of grace" (Lk 1:28). The angel greets her as if that phrase is her title: "Hail, full of grace!" Some translations render the passage "Hail, O favored one!" And translation is indeed difficult because the Greek word in question, *kecharitomene*, appears almost nowhere else in ancient literature. When the New Testament elsewhere wishes to describe someone as "filled with grace," it employs a different phrase, such as *pleres charito* in the case of Stephen (Acts 6:8).

The rarity of the word itself bespeaks the singularity of Mary's condition. The Greek grammatical form indicates that her "grace" or "favor" is a present and permanent condition resulting from a past action by God. Even the angel's form of greeting is unique in Scripture: It marks the only time an angel addresses someone by a title instead of a personal name.

Mary's kinswoman Elizabeth, inspired by God, recognizes the young girl's uniqueness as she cries out: "Blessed are you among women, and blessed is the fruit of your womb!" (Lk 1:41–42). Again, Mary—unlike the other saints we have encountered—is "blessed" in life, from the first moment we see her, and not merely in death, having "died in the Lord."

Mary herself testifies that this is only the beginning: "For behold, henceforth all generations will call me blessed" (Lk 1:48)— a statement that would have seemed unduly arrogant in the mouth of any other historical character. Very few people are remembered beyond their lifetime; hardly any are known after a thousand years. Yet the Bible itself has canonized the outlandish claim of this poor Nazarene village girl.

And Mary's blessedness—her beatitude—is not merely a pecu-
liarity of St. Luke's Gospel. It is in the Book of Revelation as well.
At the dramatic climax of John's vision, he sees "a woman clothed
with the sun, with the moon under her feet, and on her head a
crown of twelve stars; she was with child" (Rev 12:1–2). The
woman's son is a "male child . . . who is to rule all the nations with
a rod of iron" and is "caught up to God and to His throne" (v. 5).
The child is clearly Jesus; so the radiant woman is His mother. We
then see Mary crowned in heaven, bejeweled with cosmic lights, a
blessing that is singular not only among women, but within the entire human race. And since it is heavenly it is everlasting.

Mary in the Middle?

Since Mary is one of the saints, we can apply to her all the verses
that we apply to the saints in general. We may approach her as an
intercessor and a mediator (see our discussion of 1 Tim 2:1–5,
above). St. John's Gospel even seems to emphasize her role as an intercessor. There we see that it was Mary who triggered Jesus' public ministry. She pointed out a need: the wedding feast had hardly
begun, and the newlyweds had already run out of wine. Though
Jesus gave no clear indication that He would fulfill her request, she
remained confident that He would. She said to the servants: "Do
whatever He tells you" (Jn 2:5). And Jesus turned their jars full of
water into the finest wine.

In this story more than any other story of the saints, we see that
intercessory prayer does not distract us from Christ or detract from
His work. The bottom line for Mary, as for all the saints, is this:
"Do whatever He tells you." That's the way the saints themselves
lived their lives, and that's why we look to them for help as we live
our own lives.

And can we doubt that their prayers are efficacious? We have to acknowledge that, in this case at least, a request from Mary set in motion a three-year spree of miracles and wonders.

Still, skeptics may ask if Jesus intended her to occupy that place in our lives ever afterward. To answer that, we must turn from the beginning of our Lord's public ministry to the end. When He hung dying on the cross, Jesus could look down on just a handful of disciples who had remained with Him to the end (see Jn 19:26). One was His mother, Mary; another was the "disciple whom He loved," whom tradition identifies as the apostle John. Crucifixion is a slow death by intermittent suffocation, so Jesus was unable to speak much to them. Every word cost Him His life's breath and caused Him immense pain. So we can be sure that He made every word count. Among the few pronouncements He made from the cross was this: He turned to His mother and said, "Woman, behold your son!"—indicating the beloved disciple standing nearby. Then He turned to John and said, "Behold your mother!"

"And from that hour," the Gospel tells us, "the disciple took her to his own home" (Jn 19:27).

We should attend very carefully to that scene, at least because it was Jesus' final instruction before His death. It was, in a sense, a last will and testament. At the cross, John stood as a representative figure, because we are all Jesus' "beloved disciples." That may be why he never mentioned his own name during the course of his Gospel. He wanted us to walk with Jesus, as beloved disciples, each of us in John's place.

So when John received Mary as his mother, he was receiving her as *our* mother, too. The cross is a decisive moment for us. It marks our incorporation into God's family. Because of the cross, we can share Jesus' life. We are His brothers. We can share His home in heaven. We can share His Father: God!

And so all of us, all His "beloved disciples," can share His mother, too. Since Christ is our brother, His Father is our Father. His home is our home. And His mother is our mother. That is how we approach her in intercessory prayer.

Nevertheless, some people will quote two Scripture verses where Jesus Himself seems to deprecate His own mother. First there is this, from Luke:

> Then His mother and His brothers came to Him, but they
> could not reach Him for the crowd. And He was told,
> "Your mother and your brother are standing outside,
> desiring to see You." But He said to them, "My mother and
> My brothers are those who hear the word of God and do
> it." (Lk 8:19–21).

The second passage takes us back to the wedding feast at Cana, in John's Gospel:

> When the wine failed, the mother of Jesus said to Him,
> "They have no wine." And Jesus said to her, "O woman,
> what have you to do with Me? My hour has not yet come."
> (Jn 2:3–4).

Used in this way, these passages are simply red herrings. In the first case, Jesus said nothing disrespectful. He simply pointed out that His spiritual family shares His life and follows His ways. As we saw in the first chapter of Luke's Gospel, Mary was the person par excellence who heard the word of God, accepted it (Lk 1:38), and carried it out. Her biological relationship with Jesus was dependent upon that fact. And for that reason, more than for her blood kinship with Him, she was Jesus' mother.

As for the second passage: Although calling someone "woman" might offend the standards of modern etiquette, it was a sign of respect and affection in the ancient world (see Jn 4:21, 8:10). It is likely, too, that John was portraying the Cana episode as a reversal of the fall of Adam and Eve in Genesis. Thus, as Christ is the new Adam, so Mary is placed in the role of a new Eve. As Adam called Eve "woman" (Gen 2:23), so Christ addresses Mary with the same title. Moreover, in Genesis, God speaks of a future woman whose son would trample the devil underfoot (Gen 3:15), and that son could only be Jesus.

Then what about that strange phrase, "What have you to do with Me?" It is a Hebrew figure of speech that can mean many different things. Since Mary's confidence never wavers, she clearly does not hear it as a sign of disrespect or refusal.

Yet there is a still more important reason why we know that Jesus meant no disrespect toward His mother. It is because we know He was perfectly obedient to the law, and the law of Moses commands everyone to "Honor your father and mother." The Hebrew verb translated as "honor" can also mean "to bestow glory." The New Testament has shown us, again and again, that Jesus bestowed unique glories upon His mother: blessings, graces, answered prayers, and His nearest physical presence, His physical indwelling!

Jesus Christ was the only person in history who could create His own mother. He kept the law by honoring her as He made her, and He fulfilled the law by honoring her at the end of her earthly days.

We Christians are called to imitate Christ; and so we, too, honor Mary. We honor her as His mother, and we honor her as our own. We don't honor her *instead of* Him. Our honor for her is itself an expression of our devotion to Him.

VESSEL OF HONOR

Christ honored His mother. That is the key to understanding the ancient Christian doctrines regarding Mary, especially her immaculate conception, her perpetual virginity, and her bodily assumption into heaven.

Do you remember the literal meaning of "holiness" in the Hebrew word *kiddushin*? It means "set apart." The golden vessels of the Jerusalem Temple were set apart for use in worship. You could not take home the holy lampstands, for example, and use them to light up your dining room. Nor could you use the plate that held the bread of the presence in any place but its ritual setting. These things were set apart for a divine purpose. That is the meaning of their holiness.

Mary, too, was set apart. She was the lamp that bore the Light of the World. Her body contained not just the bread of presence, but the very Bread of Life. God prepared her for this purpose by coming to her while she was a virgin; and He honored her role by preserving her virginity throughout her life. This is not a denigration of sexuality, any more than the reservation of ritual vessels was a denigration of gold. It is a recognition of special purpose.

Mary was to be filled with Christ and only with Christ. That is the meaning of *her* holiness. In the Eastern churches, she is called the *Panagia*, the All-Holy. This is another way of calling her "full of grace," as the angel addressed her in Luke's Gospel. She is so brimming with grace—with God's life—that there is no room for anything else. Everything in her is holy. So, like the Temple vessels, she could not be returned to ordinary earthly use. She remained "perpetually virgin." She had no sexual relations with her husband, Joseph. She had no children after Jesus. This has been the constant faith of Christians. It was held firmly by the classic reformers, including Martin Luther, John Calvin, Ulrich Zwingli, and John Wesley.

Some modern Christians object (as did one ancient) that the Gospels refer to "the brothers of the Lord." But the text is inconclusive. In tribal cultures, all familial relations—but especially one's nearest kinfolk—are considered "brothers" and "sisters." Neither the Hebrew nor the Aramaic language had a word for "cousin" or "distant relation." The custom of calling cousins "brother" or "sister" has continued in many places in the Middle East and Africa, even today.

Nor does Jesus' title of "firstborn" require other children of Mary in the natural order. It was a technical term in Jewish law, used to describe the one who "opened" the mother's womb—whether or not other children followed.

Finally, if the "brothers of the Lord" were indeed Mary's children, it is highly unlikely that Jesus would have entrusted her care to the apostle John, as He did on the cross (Jn 19:26–27).

ALL HOLY

As Mary was reserved to God in her procreative powers, even more was she preserved from sin. That is why John's Gospel presents her as a "new Eve"—because Eve was the only other woman who had been created free from humankind's heritage of sin. To be "full of grace" is to be without sin; for the locus of sin would be devoid of grace. From the first moment of her life, Mary was preserved from sin. Christian tradition calls this her "immaculate conception."

Against Catholic claims of Mary's sinlessness, critics will sometimes cite St. Paul: "all have sinned and fall short of the glory of God" (Rom 3:23). But this proof-text really proves nothing. In English we use the word "all" in many ways. It can represent a universal collective (meaning "all of all sorts"). It can represent a more restricted collective (meaning "all of some sort"). Or it can be simply distributive (meaning "some of all sorts").

In Romans 3:23, Paul is arguing against the Judaizers by showing them, from several Old Testament passages, that it wasn't only gentiles who were under sin's power but many Jews, too. The Greek word translated as "all" (*pas*) is used in a distributive sense, meaning many gentiles and many Jews. It does not mean "everyone without exception." In fact, it *cannot* mean a universal collective of everyone—for it cannot include Jesus, who was sinless. Nor can it include babies who die in infancy and never have the opportunity to commit a personal sin.

Much later in the same Letter to the Romans, St. Paul uses a form of *pas* when he writes that the Roman Christians are "filled with all [*pases*] knowledge." He certainly doesn't mean that they're omniscient, as only God truly has "all knowledge." He just means that they possess wisdom of all sorts.

In the case of humanity's sinfulness, we can say that the sense of "all" in Romans 3:23 is indeed very strong, though still not comprehensive. Jesus Himself would be one necessary exception to the statement. Christians have always believed that Mary is the second exception. St. Augustine had this to say in 415 A.D.: "Now with the exception of the holy Virgin Mary in regard to whom, out of respect for the Lord, I do not propose to have a single question raised on the subject of sin . . . with the exception of this Virgin, if we could bring together into one place all those holy men and women, while they lived here, and ask them whether they were without sin, what are we to suppose that they would have replied?"

Other critics will object that Mary's sinlessness means that she did not stand in need of a Savior. But that doesn't necessarily follow. In fact, Mary calls God her Savior in St. Luke's Gospel (1:47). There are two ways a person can be saved from danger, by intervention and by prevention. Some people are saved after years of drug addiction, for example, by intervention and rehabilitation. Many others, however, are saved from addiction because they are spared the temptation: they are raised in good homes and kept out of harm's way. Mary was uniquely saved from all sin by preservation; but it was God who did the saving.

To Him be the glory—whenever we glorify the mother He made for Himself.

Eight

A MASS OF EVIDENCE

On the Eucharist and the
Purifying Fire of Sacrifice

To Roman Catholics, the Mass occupies a central place in life. It is the "breaking of the bread" found throughout the Acts of the Apostles and identified as a distinguishing sign of Christian life (Acts 2:42). It is the ubiquitous "pure offering" foretold by the Prophet Malachi (1:11). It is the fulfillment of Jesus' explicit command at the Last Supper (Lk 22:19).

So Catholics are often dumbfounded when critics say that the Mass is a "fourth-century invention" (as I saw in one tract) or "unbiblical." These charges seem so patently absurd that an unprepared Catholic hardly knows where to begin.

There are many ways to respond, but almost all of them fall under one of two principles, which we'd all do well to remember:

1. The Mass is saturated with the Bible.
2. The Bible is saturated with the Mass.

This topic is so large that we could write several books and still hardly scratch the surface. (In fact, I already have!) But let's consider the scriptural character of the Mass using these two principles as our guides.

The Bible in the Mass

It's easy to see why Catholics respond with incredulity when people say the Mass is unbiblical. Their experience of the Mass flatly contradicts the charge. *Reality* contradicts the charge.

In every Mass there are at least three full Bible readings, chosen from the Old and New Testaments. The Church prescribes particular readings for every day of a three-year cycle. Over the course of that period, Catholics attending daily Mass will hear most of the content of most of the books of the Bible. Catholics attending Mass on Sundays and holy days (such as Christmas, the Lord's Ascension, and so on) will hear all the Bible's key passages repeatedly proclaimed.

The first reading at a typical Mass is drawn from either the Old Testament or one of the non-Gospel New Testament books—that is, the Acts of the Apostles, the epistles, or the Book of Revelation. After the first reading, the congregation recites or sings one of the Psalms. Then, the priest or deacon reads a passage from the Gospels. On certain holy days, such as Palm Sunday and Easter Vigil, the congregation reads even longer passages from even more books of the Bible.

As a man who spent his first thirty years attending Protestant churches—and served as a Presbyterian minister—I can testify that the Catholic Church proclaims a much greater quantity of Scripture, much more consistently, than any other Christian body I know. By specifying the readings for every Sunday—and indeed every day of the week—the Catholic Church asks its preachers to present the whole biblical story to their congregations. In contrast, I, as a Protestant preacher, never preached on the Book of the Prophet Zephaniah. It's not that I had anything against Zephaniah, but my denomination tended to present only one Bible reading per service, and I could always find passages more important and interesting than anything in Zephaniah. Yet Zephaniah is the inspired and inerrant word of God; and, as such, it should be preached. As a Protestant I could have agreed with that assertion, but still never have found an opportune time to preach it. The Catholic Church, on the other hand, makes sure that a representative sample of the entire Bible reaches the people, and always in due season.

And there is still more of the Bible included in every Mass. Many of the standard prayers are taken verbatim from the pages of Scripture. Consider just a sampling.

Opening blessing	Mt 28:19
Apostolic greeting	2 Cor 13:14
Amen	1 Chr 16:36b
The Lord be with you.	Lk 1:28; 2 Thess 3:16; Ruth 2:4
Lord, have mercy.	Mt 17:15, 20:31; Ps 123:3
Glory to God . . .	Lk 2:14, plus many texts in Revelation
Alleluia	Rev 19:1–6; Tob 13:18
Lift up your hearts.	Lam 3:41
Holy, holy, holy . . .	Rev 4:8; Is 6:3; Mk 11:9–10; Ps 118:26
Eucharistic prayer	1 Cor 11:23–26; Mt 26:26–28; Mk 14:22–24; Lk 22:17–20
The great amen	Rev 5:14
The Lord's Prayer	Mt 6:9–13
Peace be with you.	Jn 14:27; 20:19

Lamb of God	Jn 1:29; Rev 5:6 and elsewhere
This is the Lamb of God . . .	Rev 19:9
Lord, I am not worthy . . .	Mt 8:8
Go in peace.	Lk 7:50; 2 Chr 35:3
Thanks be to God.	2 Cor 9:15

Add to these the congregational hymns, whose lyrics are usually biblical, and you'll find that—short of just reading the Bible aloud for an hour—the Mass couldn't get more biblical.

Yet it does! For the gestures of the Mass are biblical, too, and so are the furnishings and even the wardrobe. Catholic worship tracks very closely with the heavenly worship as it is portrayed in the Book of Revelation. When the priest makes the sign of the cross, he is making the mark described in Revelation 7:3 and 14:1 and foreshadowed in Ezekiel 9:4. When he stretches out his arms, he evokes Moses during the Battle with Amalek (Ex 17:12) and Jesus on the cross. At the end of Mass, when the priest extends his hands, he is doing what priests have done since the days of Israel's sojourn in the desert: "Then Aaron lifted up his hands toward the people and blessed them" (Lev 9:22).

The early Christians, such as Ignatius of Antioch and Tertullian, recognized that the Church established its altars on earth in order to imitate heaven's altar (see Rev 8:3). The Church's priests wear vestments in order to imitate the robed presbyters who worship in heaven (see Rev 4:4). And even in the age of electric lights, the Church continues to use candles in order to evoke the lampstands depicted in the Bible's most vivid heavenly visions (Rev 1:12). The same is true of the use of incense in worship (see Rev 5:8) and chalices (Rev 16) as vessels.

Congregational kneeling, practiced in the Western Church, is another Gospel practice. In the New Testament, kneeling is the prayer posture of mothers, rulers, lepers, and Jesus Himself (Mt 8:2, 9:18, 15:25; Lk 22:41). With a pedigree like that, it's hard to argue against the posture.

Nevertheless, some people will. They'll say that these practices follow the letter and not the spirit of the New Testament, that they are evidence not of religion but of ritualism and ceremonialism. But such charges are untrue. Christian worship does indeed involve rituals and ceremonies, but the Gospel does not forbid rituals and ceremonies. In fact, the New Testament prescribes several important rituals and *commands* Christians to perform them: baptism (Mt 28:19), the Eucharist (Lk 22:19), anointing (Jas 5:14), confession of sins (Jas 5:16), and the ordination of clergy (1 Tim 4:14). Faithful to God's word, the Catholic Church continues to exercise all these rites.

This is neither ritualism nor ceremonialism. A practice becomes an *–ism* only when people make it an end in itself. But these rites are not ends in themselves. God Himself established them for our good, and they are ordered to His worship.

THE MASS IN THE BIBLE

Make no mistake about it: the Mass is the Church's fulfillment of an explicit command of Jesus Christ, an important command issued at a pivotal moment in His ministry, a command recorded in the Gospel and in one of St. Paul's letters. Here it is in its earliest recorded form:

> For I received from the Lord what I also delivered to you,
> that the Lord Jesus on the night when He was betrayed
> took bread, and when He had given thanks, He broke it,
> and said, "This is My body which is for you. Do this in

remembrance of Me." In the same way also the cup, after
supper, saying, "This cup is the new covenant in My blood.
Do this, as often as you drink it, in remembrance of Me."
(I Cor 11:23–25)

A command cannot get much simpler or more direct than that:
Just do it.

And so the early Christians *did*, wherever they went. I have already mentioned the passage from Acts (2:42, 46) where Luke lists
"the breaking of the bread" among the defining characteristics of
the Church. The remaining chapters of Acts bear this out, as we repeatedly see the community "do this" in remembrance of Jesus
(see, for example, Acts 20:7 and 27:35). In Acts 13:2 we find the
public worship of the Church described by a word familiar to
Catholics, and that is "liturgy" (from the Greek root *leitourgia*). We
see, in that passage, that the Apostles, like modern Catholics, fasted
for the celebration of the Mass.

What Jesus did, and what He commanded the Apostles to do,
Catholics continue to do today.

Like so many other details in the life of Jesus, this one was foretold and foreshadowed in the Old Testament. The Church's Eucharistic prayers emphasize this by mentioning the sacrifices of
Abel and Abraham and the bread and wine offered by
Melchizedek. We have already seen that the Church Fathers saw the
universality of the Mass as a fulfillment of the prophet Malachi's
"pure offering," from east to west (Mal 1:11). The Fathers also
cherished the Mass as the fulfillment of a "Wisdom's banquet" of
bread and wine (Prv 9:1–6), and as the true wayfarer's bread signified by the angel's feeding of the prophet Elijah (I Kgs 19:5–7).
As the Israelites revered the bread of the presence (Ex 25:29) and
drew holiness from it (Lev 24:9), so the Church worshiped the

Real Presence in the Eucharist and experienced it as a source of grace.

Jesus taught that the Eucharist was foreshadowed in the manna given by God during Israel's exodus from Egypt (see Jn 6:49–51). Indeed, long before the Last Supper, Jesus Himself foreshadowed the Eucharist by multiplying bread to feed His congregations, by repeatedly evoking banquet scenes in His preaching, and by choosing to be born in a town named Bethlehem (Hebrew for "House of Bread"). In an extended, explicit foretelling, He detailed the theology of His Eucharistic presence in the famous "Bread of Life" discourse (Jn 26–58). "I am the living bread which came down from heaven; if any one eats of this bread, he will live for ever; and the bread which I shall give for the life of the world is My flesh" (Jn 6:51). His flesh is bread; His blood is drink. This corresponds directly to His pronouncements over the bread and wine at the Last Supper: "This is My Body . . . This is the cup of My blood"—the very action He commanded His Apostles to repeat.

It is a curious fact that those who ordinarily insist on a strictly literal reading of the Bible will, with equal insistence, interpret these passages exclusively in terms of metaphor. (This is what I myself did, many years ago.) Yet Jesus did not treat "bread" and "blood" and "flesh" as metaphors. In the Bread of Life discourse, His language shocked His hearers. The verbs are more graphic in the Greek; He's telling the assembly that they must "chew" or "gnaw" His flesh. Yet, the more the people expressed their disgust, the more graphic and realistic Jesus' language became.

"Many of His disciples, when they heard it, said, 'This is a hard saying; who can listen to it?' " (Jn 6:60). This is true not only of the people who gathered around Jesus that day in Capernaum, but also of many Christians throughout history. It seems outlandish and unseemly for God to command believers to eat His flesh and drink His blood. It seems at least odd for Him to prescribe bread to be the object of their chief act of worship. But so He did. And so, in subsequent generations, Christians would endure unjust charges of cannibalism from their Roman persecutors, but they would not deny Jesus' bodily presence in the Eucharist. And so Catholics today endure even the jeers of other Christians, but we stand by the unequivocal words of the New Testament.

"Jesus, knowing in Himself that His disciples murmured at it, said to them, 'Do you take offense at this?' " (Jn 6:61). He went on to say, "the flesh is of no avail"; but even this provides no easy way past His realistic language, because He was not speaking here of His own flesh—which certainly availed us our salvation!

Jesus has left no loophole. With St. Peter, the Catholic must answer, "Lord, to whom shall we go? You have the words of eternal life" (Jn 6:68). We hear those "words of life"—and we see them embodied as the Bread of Life—in every Mass we attend.

For the Mass is an earthly sharing in eternal life—an earthly participation in heaven's worship. The first Christians, like Catholics today, based this belief on the New Testament Letter to the Hebrews and the Book of Revelation. Both books are saturated with images of ritual worship. We have been summoned to "the city of the living God, the heavenly Jerusalem, and to innumerable angels in festal gathering, and to the assembly of the firstborn who are enrolled in heaven . . . and to Jesus, the mediator of a new covenant, and to the sprinkled blood that speaks more graciously than the blood of Abel" (Heb 12:22–24). This is the ancient and perennial Catholic understanding of the Mass.

The Book of Revelation further describes this assembly as the "marriage supper of the Lamb" (Rev 19:9). The supper takes place at heaven's altar (Rev 8:3), where chalices are poured out (Rev 14:10). In Revelation as in Paul's First Letter to the Corinthians, we see that the Eucharistic chalices are cups of blessing for the faithful, but cups of wrath for sinners (see I Cor 11:28–30).

When Catholics go to Mass, they drink from the "blessing cup . . . a communion in the blood of Christ" (I Cor 10:16). They go to heaven, as John did when he was in the Spirit on the Lord's Day, and as the Corinthian Christians did when they "assemble[d] as a Church" (I Cor 11:18). The first Christians were "the assembly of the firstborn . . . enrolled in heaven." And so are we!

The Mass as Sacrifice

Yet we know we are not yet worthy of heaven. That is why we are dependent upon the chalice we receive in the Mass, the blood of Jesus, whose "sprinkled blood . . . speaks more graciously than the blood of Abel." The blood of Christ—the cup of His blood—purifies sinners who are repentant; it is, for them, a chalice of blessing and forgiveness.

The Catholic Church teaches that Holy Communion removes all venial sins from the soul of the sinner. Through our contact with Jesus, we become by grace what He is by nature. We partake of His nature. He is all-pure, all-holy, and so His touch purifies us. What He said to the leper is equally true for us: "I will; be clean" (Mt 8:3).

In the Old Covenant, the Israelites offered sacrifices to atone for sins. But now Christ has become the all-sufficing sacrifice. By His death, He accomplished what all the many millions of offerings of the ancient world could never accomplish. Listen to the Epistle to the Hebrews: "For if the sprinkling of defiled persons with the blood of goats and bulls and with the ashes of a heifer sanctifies for the purification of the flesh, how much more shall the blood of Christ, who through the eternal Spirit offered Himself without blemish to God, purify your conscience from dead works to serve the living God" (9:13–14). Christ's death and resurrection mark a "once-for-all" sacrifice: "we have been sanctified through the offering of the body of Jesus Christ once for all" (Heb 9:10).

Jesus' dying and rising happened just once in history. But He willed a way for all people, in all ages, to participate in that sacrifice. That God-willed way is the Mass, which itself is the sacrifice of Jesus Christ. He is not "killed again and again," as some critics claim. But He is offered continuously, a pure offering, from the rising of the sun to its setting.

Christ's sacrifice does not negate ours, but makes it possible. Indeed, it was Jesus who commanded His ministerial priests to participate in His sacrificial action. It was He who said, "Do this in remembrance of Me." His Apostles, like all subsequent Catholic priests, did not *substitute* themselves for Jesus, but rather *represented* Him and *participated* in His priesthood.

The first Christians lived in a world where sacrifice was a common part of religion. If they had converted from Judaism, they knew the sacrifices of the Jerusalem Temple. If they had converted from paganism, they knew the sacrifices to pagan deities. But now all those sacrifices gave way to the rite they habitually called "*the* sacrifice." Hebrews quotes Psalm 50:23 to encourage a continual "sacrifice of praise" (Heb 13:15) in the Church. Paul commonly uses the language of sacrificial worship—words such as *leitourgia* (liturgy; e.g., Phil 2:17), *eucharistia* (thanksgiving, eucharist; e.g., 2 Cor 9:11), *thusia* (sacrifice; e.g., Phil 4:18), *hierourgein* (priestly service; e.g., Rom 15:16), and *prosphoron* (offering; e.g., Rom 15:16). Peter speaks of the entire Church as a priesthood called to "offer sacrifices acceptable to God through Jesus Christ" (1 Pet 2:5).

That sacrificial language appears also in the writings of the Christians who were disciples of the Apostles. The ancient book called the *Didache* repeatedly uses the word "sacrifice" to describe the Eucharist: "And on the Lord's own day gather yourselves together and break bread and give thanks, first confessing your transgressions, that your sacrifice may be pure." St. Ignatius of Antioch, writing only a few years after the death of the Apostles, habitually referred to the Church as "the place of sacrifice."

In the Old Testament, sacrifices initiated or restored communion between God and man. So, in the New Testament, does the sacrifice of the Mass, only more perfectly. For St. Ignatius and his contemporaries in 105 A.D., the Church was united in communion by the Eucharist. This they had learned well from St. Paul, who said: "Because there is one bread, we who are many are one body, for we all partake of the one bread" (I Cor 10:17). Ignatius clarified this doctrine for anyone who might be in doubt: "Take heed, then, to have but one Eucharist. For there is one flesh of our Lord Jesus Christ, and one cup to show forth the unity of His blood; one altar; as there is one bishop, along with the priests and deacons, my fellow-servants." Ignatius defined heretics as those who "refrain from the Eucharist and from prayer, because they do not confess that the Eucharist is the flesh of our Savior Jesus Christ, which suffered for our sins, and which the Father in His goodness raised up."

Because we have not grown up around sacrifical cults, as the first Christians did, we might not recognize that Ignatius is everywhere using the language of sacrifice—when he speaks of an altar, for example, and the offering of flesh. In another of his letters, he even compares himself to an offering of wheat and of bread. Every sacrificial cult—whether in Israel or Greece or Rome—required a priesthood. A priest is, by definition, someone who offers sacrifice (see Heb 8:3). Ignatius recognizes the priesthood of all believers, as does St. Peter; but he also recognizes, as did St. Paul, that certain men are set apart to preside over the rites of the Church. Ignatius wrote the Smyrnaeans: "Let that eucharist alone be considered valid which is celebrated in the presence of the bishop, or of him to whom he shall have entrusted it."

In Revelation, the New Testament book that Catholics have called an "icon of the liturgy," Christ appears as a sacrificial lamb (Rev 5:6). It is the blood of this Lamb, given in sacrifice, that "takes away the sins of the world" (Jn 1:29).

Now the offering is in heaven, right where John saw it. But heaven touches down to earth in the Mass. The Church Fathers liked to quote the Prophet Isaiah when they spoke about the Eucharisic sacrifice and its power to take away sins: "Then flew one of the seraphim to me, having in his hand a burning coal which he had taken with tongs from the altar. And he touched my mouth, and said: 'Behold, this has touched your lips; your guilt is taken away, and your sin forgiven' " (Is 6:6–7). For the early Christians, that "burning coal" foreshadowed the Blessed Sacrament, the bread come down from heaven's altar to purify the Church at prayer.

MASSES FOR THE DEAD

The purifying sacrifice is what we want to keep in mind when our non-Catholic friends ask us why we offer votive Masses for the dead. There are many questions bound up with this one.

The first question is whether anything we do—any work of ours—can actually be redemptive for another person. According to St. Paul, the answer is yes. "For we are God's fellow workers" (I Cor 3:9). God willed that we should cooperate in His work of redemption. St. Paul went on to say: "in my flesh I complete what is lacking in Christ's afflictions for the sake of His body, that is, the

Church" (Col 1:24). God willed that we should not only work out our own salvation (see Phil 2:12), but also "Bear one another's burdens" (Gal 6:2) as we share in Christ's redemptive sacrifice. We can and should intercede for one another, for the remission of one another's sins. "If anyone sees his brother committing what is not a mortal sin, he will ask, and God will give him life for those whose sin is not mortal" (I Jn 5:16).

A further question is whether we can do anything for a person already dead. Many Protestants will say no, because our disposition at death gives only two possibilities: heaven or hell. If a person's going to heaven, then the strife is over and that's that. For those who are going to hell, there's nothing we can do to change their course. Their lifetime was the trial period, and it's over.

The traditional Christian view is indeed binary. At death, our souls are bound heavenward or bound for hell. But, since "nothing unclean shall enter" heaven (Rev 21:27), we need first to be purified. From reflection on Scripture, the Church has always taught that there is an intermediate state for those who are bound for heaven; it is a state of purification; and tradition calls it purgatory.

Where do we find it in the Bible? It is implied in many places. Jesus assumes the doctrine when He says: "whoever says a word against the Son of man will be forgiven; but whoever speaks against the Holy Spirit will not be forgiven, either in this age or in the age to come" (Mt 12:32). There must be a state, then, in which people are forgiven "in the age to come." Tradition calls that state purgatory.

In another place, Jesus is speaking of God's judgment. He says: "Make friends quickly with your accuser, while you are going with him to court, lest your accuser hand you over to the judge, and the judge to the guard, and you be put in prison; truly, I say to you, you will never get out till you have paid the last penny" (Mt 5:25–26).

Again, this implies a state in the afterlife in which people "pay" their penitential debt to God—that is, they are purified. And Christian tradition calls that state purgatory.

Even in the Old Testament the prophets discussed judgment in these terms. Malachi employed the image that will recur in the New Testament. The final purification of the faithful, he says, is like a refiner's fire. "But who can endure the day of His coming, and who can stand when He appears? For He is like a refiner's fire and like fullers' soap; He will sit as a refiner and purifier of silver, and He will purify the sons of Levi and refine them like gold and silver" (Mal 3:2–3).

St. Paul, too, speaks of this purifying fire. It is the fire of those who are ultimately saved, not damned. Indeed, Paul says the fire itself is their salvation, for it rids them of the sins that cannot enter heaven. Paul's explanation is worth quoting at length:

Each man's work will become manifest; for the Day will disclose it, because it will be revealed with fire, and the fire will test what sort of work each one has done. If the work which any man has built on the foundation survives, he will receive a reward. If any man's work is burned up, he will suffer loss, though he himself will be saved, but only as through fire.

That saving fire is what Catholics call purgatory.

The Book of Revelation makes a distinction between the martyrs who are resurrected immediately and "rest of the dead" who "did not come to life until the thousand years were ended" (Rev 20:5). We see that some were judged worthy of heaven, but others weren't ready yet for their inevitable resurrection to glory. Their state of purification is purgatory.

There is an intermediate state between earth and heaven. The Israelites called it *Sheol*, the abode of the dead. And the Jews of Jesus' time fervently believed that the souls of God's faithful could be "delivered . . . from the depths of Sheol" (Ps 86:13). Pious Jews, then as now, considered it an obligation to raise prayers (the *Kaddish*) for their deceased family members. They could even offer a sacrifice for the sake of the faithful departed. Consider this story, of the aftermath of a battle, a little over a century and a half before Jesus' birth.

> Judas [Maccabeus] and his men went to take up the bodies of the fallen and to bring them back to lie with their kinsmen in the sepulchres of their fathers. Then under the tunic of every one of the dead they found sacred tokens of the idols of Jamnia, which the law forbids the Jews to wear. And it became clear to all that this was why these men had fallen. So they all blessed the ways of the Lord, the righteous Judge, who reveals the things that are hidden; and they turned to prayer, beseeching that the sin which had been committed might be wholly blotted out. And the noble Judas . . . took up a collection, man by man, to the amount of two thousand drachmas of silver, and sent it to Jerusalem to provide for a sin offering. In doing this he acted very well and honorably, taking account of the resurrection. For if he were not expecting that those who had fallen would rise again, it would have been superfluous and foolish to pray for the dead. But if he was looking to the splendid reward that is laid up for those who fall asleep in godliness, it was a holy and pious thought. Therefore he made atonement for the dead, that they might be delivered from their sin. (2 Mac 12:39–45)

The soldiers offered sacrifice for their fallen comrades. They offered a "sin offering" to atone for the sins of the dead—sins that the survivors had not themselves committed. And when they did this, they acted in a holy, pious, and honorable way.

Protestants do not consider the account of the Maccabean Revolt to be part of the canonical Scriptures. Catholics do. But even those who do not accept it as Scripture will find it to be a valuable historical witness—a glimpse of the beliefs of Jews in Jesus' time—the beliefs implied in Jesus' own statements about an intermediate state in the afterlife. This is the "prison" of spirits where, according to St. Peter, Jesus first went to preach the Good News (I Pet 3:19–20). The Jews called it *Sheol.* The Greek New Testament calls it *Hades* (as distinct from *Gehenna*, the place of hellfire). Catholics call it purgatory.

The early Christians knew that, if the Old Testament sacrifices had been efficacious on behalf of the dead, Jesus' sacrifice would be all the more powerful. So they commonly offered graveside Masses on the third day after a Christian's burial—the third day, as a sign of Easter hope. Some churches offered graveside Masses on the seventh day, the ninth, the thirtieth, and the fortieth as well. In St. Augustine's autobiography, the *Confessions* (written in the fourth century), he recalled how his mother's dying request was that he should remember her when he offered the Mass.

Catholics know how much God's mercy radiates through this doctrine. Our Masses for the dead give healing, not only to the dead, but also to the living who must go on in grief. When we bid good-bye to a loved one, we often wish we could have done more for them. The Good News—the Gospel truth—is that we can. We can give them all we have to give, which (thank God) is all that Jesus has to give. We can give them the once-for-all sacrifice of the Mass.

Nine

PEACE OF THE ROCK

On the Papal Office and Its Paper Trail

As I said earlier, there was a time in my life when I came—after some struggle—to accept the biblical basis of the Catholic claim for honoring the saints in heaven.

But I drew the line there, at the afterlife. The saints in heaven, I reasoned, are safely dead. We can revere them then without fear of their abusing the privilege. I bristled, however, at the thought of showing reverence or deference to a living authority. And no one on earth so exemplified that kind of authority as the pope.

To Catholics, he is the supreme pontiff, the Vicar of Christ, the Bishop of Rome, the Holy Father. The pope considers himself to be the Servant of the Servants of God.

But to me, as for many Protestants, he represented the office we were united in rejecting. We might vehemently disagree with one another about the merits of infant versus adult baptism, about freedom of the human will, about the mode of Christ's presence in the Lord's Supper, and about predestination. But we agreed on one point: our disagreement with the papacy.

Obedience to the pope, respect for his office, kissing his ring, receiving his blessing, hanging his picture, believing that he has a God-given grace of infallibility—these practices and beliefs, in my view, sailed dangerously close to idolatry. Where, I asked, was the biblical warrant for such behavior and such belief?

Because the papacy was a stumbling block for me—and it is a perennial lightning rod for criticism by non-Catholics—I want to spend a short chapter discussing it here and then return to it later in the book. In this chapter, I'll respond to some common objections against Catholic doctrine on the papacy. I'm reserving a more substantive (and positive) biblical treatment of the subject for later in the book, when we discuss God's kingdom and the Church.

QUICK Q&A

In discussions of the papacy, there arise common objections that require only short responses, because they're simply not true. They're misunderstandings in most cases, urban legends in others.

Catholics think the pope is sinless.

No, we don't. In fact, the current pope goes to confession at least once a week, as have all popes in recent memory. Presumably, they're confessing their sins, because otherwise the sacrament would not be valid. It does no good to confess one's own virtues— or someone else's sins. In the New Testament, Peter showed himself to be a sinner. This did not diminish his authority in the least.

Catholics think the pope doesn't make mistakes.

No, we don't. The popes, like all people, operate with imperfect knowledge and other human limitations. In their day-to-day living, the popes make mistakes, as we all do. Some mistakes are small, like misjudging a step in the stairwell. Other mistakes have grave consequences, like misjudging a problem in international diplomacy. The pope's grace of infallibility covers only matters of Christian faith and morals.

Catholics made up the idea of infallibility in the nineteenth century.

The doctrine was indeed fully articulated at that time, but it had been with the Church since the beginning—as in the first century, when St. Clement of Rome, a disciple of Peter and Paul, said that the Holy Spirit was speaking through him. Protestants, too, believe that God endowed certain men with infallibility, when (for example) He inspired the sacred authors to write the Scriptures. The Apostles and Evangelists wrote, with the grace of infallibility, works that were free from error. We all agree on that. Catholics and Protestants disagree only over whether the charism of infallibility has been extended beyond the first generation of Christians.

Papal authority was discredited and forfeited by the behavior of the bad popes.

No, it wasn't. Jesus faced a corrupt religious establishment in His own day; but He always affirmed their God-given authority in matters of doctrine and religious practice: "The scribes and the Pharisees sit on Moses' seat; so practice and observe whatever they tell you, but not what they do; for they preach, but do not practice"

(Mt 23:2–3). Even Caiaphas, the wicked high priest, could not help but pronounce an infallible prophecy when he was plotting Jesus' murder (see Jn 11:49–51). We should be reassured to know that, in two thousand years, very few popes have abused their power—out of 265 men, there have been only a handful of scoundrels—and God has never permitted even the scoundrels to teach error in matters of faith and morals.

If the papacy were really what Catholics say it is, there would not have been any bad popes.

Not true. Jesus gave the Apostles the grace of authority. He chose the Twelve Himself. Yet He knew that one of them would betray Him. If the apostolate were indeed what Jesus said it was, how could there be a bad Apostle? Jesus leaves everyone free to choose good or evil—even those whom He calls to sacred office.

PETER PRINCIPAL

Where, then, is our biblical justification for the papacy? Tradition relies on several texts, but one most especially. In Matthew's Gospel, Jesus asked His Apostles what sorts of things people were saying about Him. They gave Him a summary of the current rumors. Then Jesus asked them, collectively, who *they* thought He was. And Simon answered for the group:

> Simon Peter replied, "You are the Christ, the Son of the living God."
> And Jesus answered him, "Blessed are you, Simon Bar-Jona! For flesh and blood has not revealed this to you, but My Father who is in heaven. And I tell you, you are Peter,

and on this rock I will build My Church, and the powers of
death shall not prevail against it. I will give you the keys of
the kingdom of heaven, and whatever you bind on earth
shall be bound in heaven, and whatever you loose on earth
shall be loosed in heaven."

In a later chapter we will examine what "the keys" meant in the
Jewish culture of Jesus' time and place. For now, let's note a few details.

First, Simon served as the spokesman for the group, and He ut-
tered a profound doctrine: the dogma of the incarnation (see also
Jn 6:68–69). Jesus explained to Simon that such truth could not
be gained by natural means; Simon had received a special revelation
from God. And Simon, with God's help, had spoken infallibly.

Jesus then gave Simon a new name, Peter—literally, "Rock"—a
name that appears nowhere in the historical record before that moment. Jesus promised to build a divine edifice upon that rock foundation. He called the edifice "My Church"; for it would be not
merely a human institution. It would be, in some sense, incorrupt,
too: "the powers of death [or 'gates of hell'] shall not prevail
against it." So we see that God Himself gave a guarantee to preserve
Peter's authority.

Now, some critics argue that Jesus referred to Himself when He
spoke of the "rock" on which He would build His Church. They
point out that the word used for "rock" is the Greek *petra*—meaning a large rock—whereas the name He gave to Simon was the
Greek *Petros*, meaning a small rock. The critics say that Jesus meant,
essentially, that Peter was a little pebble, and Jesus was the boulder
from which the Church would rise up.

There are several problems, however, with that interpretation.
First of all, Jesus probably did not speak Greek in this exchange. It

is very likely that He spoke Aramaic, and His words were later translated into Greek when the Gospels were written. In Aramaic there is only one word that could be used for "rock": *kephas*. In Aramaic, there would have been no distinction between Peter's name and the Church's foundation.

Still, critics might press the point, noting that the Holy Spirit inspired Matthew to employ two different Greek words in his written Gospel. But Matthew did not have much choice. Jesus was speaking of a foundation stone, so *petra* would certainly be the right choice; but *petra* is a feminine noun, and so it could not have served as Simon's new name. A male could not adopt a feminine name; the name would have to be adapted, be given a masculine form. Thus, Matthew, guided by the Holy Spirit, did something that was obvious and practically necessary: he used the masculine form, *Petros*, to render Peter's name, *Kephas*.

Was Jesus giving Peter a unique role in the Church? The answer seems obvious from the remaining pages of the New Testament. As I mentioned in chapter 6, Peter is everywhere shown to be the chief spokesman, preacher, teacher, healer, judge, and administrator in the newborn Church.

Did Peter exhibit any signs of infallibility when he taught doctrine? Our critics might point out that, almost immediately after Jesus commissioned him, Peter fell; he contradicted Jesus, telling Him that He must not suffer. Jesus then reproved Peter in the strongest terms, calling him "Satan"! Our critics might note, too, that, much later in Peter's life, he found himself in conflict with Paul over the treatment of gentiles in the Church. And Paul publicly corrected Peter! Now, how could a man graced with the charism of infallibility endure public correction by both Jesus and Paul?

We should note right away that both Jesus and Paul were reproving Peter not for his *doctrine*, but for his failure of *will*. Indeed, they were faulting him for not living up to his own doctrine. In Matthew's passage, Peter had moved from confessing the Lord's divinity to rejecting the Lord's will. In the conflict with Paul, Peter had moved from eating with gentiles himself to forbidding other Jewish-Christians to practice such fellowship. Both Jesus and Paul were exhorting Peter merely to practice what he infallibly preached.

Is there a biblical justification for our calling Peter the "vicar of Christ"? Doesn't that put Peter in a place occupied by God alone? No, because Jesus Himself had said to the Apostles: "He who hears you hears Me, and he who rejects you rejects Me, and he who rejects Me rejects him who sent Me" (Lk 10:16). Jesus is clearly assigning the Twelve as His vicars. He is telling them that He will act *vicar*iously through them. And what Jesus said of all the Apostles is pre-eminently true of the Prince of Apostles, Peter. He, and his successors, would be vicars of Christ on earth. They would act with an authority that is delegated, but is truly divine.

We see this principle at work in the Acts of the Apostles. When Ananias conceals information under questioning, he is charged not with having lied to Peter (which he obviously did), but with having "lied to the Holy Spirit" (Acts 5:3). "You have lied not to men, but to God" (v. 4). As judge, Peter acted as Christ's vicar. To lie to Peter was to lie to God Himself. For Ananias, that sin was mortal in every sense. Immediately, he fell down dead.

The Buck and the Rock

Peter's authority was, in many ways, *like* the authority of the other Apostles. He shared power with them; he consulted with them; he received correction from them. Yet the buck stopped, always, with him. In Acts 1, Peter directed the apostolic college on how they should deal with the crisis of Judas's death. In Acts 11, when "the circumcision party" confronted him, Peter simply explained to them what God had shown him—and their hostility ended, immediately, without dissent, discussion, or further question. "When they heard this they were silenced" (Acts 11:18). At the Council of Jerusalem (Acts 15), it was Peter who put an end to the debate (Acts 15:7–12). He defined the doctrine, which James confirmed and further adapted (Acts 15:14–18).

If we do not accept the papal implications of the New Testament texts, we create many other problems.

Why, we may ask, would Jesus have named Peter as chief among His apostles if He had not intended the office to be, somehow, continued within the Church? It's not as if the subsequent generations needed guidance *less* than the first generation. In fact, it's arguable that we today need it more! Jesus performed this action *for our sake,* and it must have been exemplary or constitutive in some way.

Why, too, would Jesus have named Simon "rock" if He didn't intend a unique and authoritative role for him? Simon certainly didn't earn the new name by his rocklike character. He was impetuous to a fault. He wavered; he vacillated. Stability and reliability were not his strong suits. John was more steady, more reliable. Thus Jesus called John the "beloved disciple." But Jesus called Peter the rock on which He would build His Church.

Did Jesus intend that rocklike role just for Peter, or for his successors as well? We have already mentioned the crisis the Church faced upon Judas's death. They took counsel from God's word: "His office let another take" (Acts 1:20). Can we really persuade ourselves that this prerogative of succession was given to Judas, but not to Peter? I don't think so.

It is clear, in all events, that the early Christians accepted the pope's authority as Peter's, and so as Christ's. I have already mentioned Clement's exhortation that the Corinthians should "render obedience unto the things written by us through the Holy Spirit." We have already mentioned the deference that Ignatius and Irenaeus showed to Rome and the Petrine office. The witness continues in every generation afterward. Tertullian the North African said, "They have not the heritage of Peter who have not the see of Peter." In the next generation, at the beginning of the third century, St. Cyprian said "a primacy is given to Peter," and, "He who deserts the chair of Peter on whom the Church has been founded, does he still believe that he is in the Church?" Later Fathers witnessed to the pope's authority by their appeals for justice and clarification—for example, St. Basil the Great (fourth century), St. John Chrysostom (early fifth century), and St. Cyril of Alexandria (mid-fifth century).

The greatest Scripture scholar of antiquity, St. Jerome, who translated the entire Bible into Latin, hailed the pope with these words: "I speak with the successor of the fisherman and disciple of the cross. Following none but Christ as my primate, I am united in communion with Your Beatitude—that is, with the chair of Peter. Upon that Rock I know the Church is built. Whosoever eats a lamb outside this house is profane. Whoever is not in Noah's ark will perish when the flood prevails."

He put the papacy, as was his habit, in biblical terms. So should we today, when called upon to give our reasons to believe. We'll return to still more papal reasons in a few more chapters.

Ten

REASONS OF THE KINGDOM

On Answering with Your Life

When people challenge us, question us, or demand a reason for the hope we have within us, we need never be long without an answer. This doesn't mean that a wise or witty response will always come bubbling to our lips. Sometimes, our answer should be: "I don't know." There is no shame in admitting one's own ignorance, in all humility. In fact, we would offer a poor argument for the faith if we shot off our mouth in a way that misrepresented the facts, either because of our poor understanding of an issue or by our bad attitude. Remember *all* of St. Peter's admonition: "Always be prepared to make a defense to any one who calls you to account for the hope that is in you, yet *do it with gentleness and reverence*" (I Pet 3:15).

We need to hold fast to good doctrine. We need to study the general lines of the best apologetic arguments. But apologetics, by itself, is not enough. Our faith is like a fortress. Its strength depends not just on the thickness of the walls or the wideness of the moat, but most of all on the health and the resolve of the one who holds the fortress. Apologetics is concerned, above all, with our external contacts. But it depends upon on our inner strength, which is paramount. Our best defenses stand firm on the ground of our disciplined prayer life and an integrated, *theological* understanding of the Bible.

I cannot overemphasize this point. I know that *theology* is a frightening word for many people. It sometimes means stretching our minds to learn new vocabulary and new methods. It means taking up difficult material that's not always written in the most welcoming way. It requires effort, and it's a long-term project.

On the other hand, it's often easy for us to pursue apologetics. We're fueled by adrenaline when someone challenges us or insults us. We're driven by curiosity when someone asks us a question. Or we're shocked or frightened into action when someone tells us that the faith we hold dear is a deception of the devil. When we take up works of apologetics, we are usually highly motivated and seeking information for which we can find an immediate practical application. So there's, occasionally at least, instant gratification. And that's all to the good.

HEIGHTS AND DEPTHS

Still, I maintain that our best defense of Catholicism is not ad hoc or piecemeal. The Catholic Church certainly offers the most persuasive natural arguments and the most consistent biblical arguments. But the attractive power of the Catholic faith is the way it all hangs together: the natural, the biblical, and the theological. It's integrated, just as all that has come from God is recognizable as His own. The Catholic faith is as solid as the Gospel—as solid as the rock Jesus promised would uphold His Church.

Our best arguments arise not from a memorized handbook, but

from a faith that is deep and robust. We can spend a lifetime scru-
tinizing individual trees—this doctrine or those particular Bible
verses—without ever seeing the lush and verdant forest of the
Gospel. Apologetics marks a good beginning, to draw us into a
deeper and more theological relationship with God. Apologetics
marks a good end as well—an inevitable, Evangelical sharing of
what we've assimilated through prayer and study. But apologetics
should never mark the heights or depths of our knowledge of God
or our faith in His Church.

This is a quality you'll find in all the great apologetical works,
including many by the authors I mentioned in chapter 1 of this
book. They emerge from good theology, and they lead us again to
the threshold of theology.

I have sometimes heard young apologists complain about the
"sameness" of so much apologetical literature. They tire of reading
the familiar arguments again and again, with identical lists of Bible
verses to memorize. In the worst cases, they feel as if they've already learned everything there is to learn!

Whenever we feel this way, we can interpret it as a sure sign we
need to turn our focus to our life of prayer and our theological
study, even as we continue to refine our apologetic skills. For even
if we spend a lifetime in prayer and theologizing, we'll only just
skim the surface. The greatest theologian in the Church's history,
St. Thomas Aquinas, arrived at a certain point where he realized his
voluminous and brilliant work amounted only to "so much straw."
I, for my part, received my doctoral degree more than a decade ago,
and I have held prestigious chairs at various universities, but I still
feel like a beginner in this field. Every other pursuit is at least the-
oretically exhaustible. Only theology has as its essential subject
matter the infinite, the transcendent, and the eternal. The subject

might exhaust our inner resources, but we can never exhaust its inner riches.

In this book, so far, we have examined the natural reasons why Catholics believe as they do, and we have examined the biblical reasons. From here I would like to take the high road, the royal road of reasons, which are theological—though they encompass both the biblical and the natural as well. Along the way, we'll revisit some of the arguments we encountered in earlier chapters, but we'll see them, as it were, from above.

Our approach will be that of biblical theology.

HOME ECONOMICS

Biblical theology differs, in some important ways, from what is usually called "systematic theology." But the important difference for us is this: While the ordering principle behind *systematic theology* is the logical progression of doctrines, the ordering principle behind *biblical theology* is the divine economy.

What's the divine economy? The word economy comes from the Greek *oikonomia*, which means the "law of the household." The divine economy, then, is the law of God's household. Sometimes, the word is translated into English as "plan," as when St. Paul speaks of "the plan [*oikonomia*] of the mystery hidden for ages in God who created all things" (Eph 3:9). The *Catechism of the Catholic Church* defines the divine economy as "all the works by which God reveals Himself and communicates His life" (n. 236). Such works, for us, should mean all of revelation and all of creation—our natural reasons and our biblical reasons—because God is the principal author of the book of nature and the book of Scripture (CCC 117, 304).

Because God is the principal author of the Bible, we may read the entire canon as a single book, with a certain narrative unity, a plot. We may invoke Exodus, the Psalms, and the Song of Songs to illuminate John's Gospel. We can find a narrative thread that runs from the first pages of Genesis to the last pages of Revelation—and then continues through our lives today—again because the same God who authors Scripture also authored the world and its history.

I propose that we look at the entire Bible—and even all creation—through a single lens. And I propose that we trace the biblical narrative using the term that Jesus Himself used to describe the narrative's dramatic climax. I propose that we look at salvation history as the story of a *kingdom*.

The arrival of the kingdom, after all, was the theme that Jesus Himself placed at the heart of the Gospel. From the beginning of His public ministry, He proclaimed, "The time is fulfilled, and the kingdom of God is at hand" (Mk 1:15); "the kingdom of God has come upon you" (Mt 12:28). For the first Christians, the kingdom was a *present* reality, already brought about by Jesus (see, for example, Col 1:13; 1 Thess 2:12; Rev 1:6, 9, and 5:10).

Jesus announced the kingdom, but it had long been prepared and long expected. In the following chapters, we'll see how that kingdom was established, then lost, then gradually, partially restored—only to be lost again!—before its definitive fulfillment in Jesus. If we wish to understand the heart of the Gospel, we must understand what God promised in the kingdom, what He prepared and foreshadowed, and what Jesus fulfilled.

III

Royal Reasons

Eleven

CREATED FOR THE KINGDOM

In the moments before Jesus' Ascension into heaven, there is just one question burning in the hearts of the disciples: "Lord, will You at this time restore the kingdom to Israel?" (Acts 1:6).

There is, at the heart of the biblical story—and so in the hearts of God's people—a keen sense of loss and gain, fall and redemption. God had bestowed a kingdom on His people. They forfeited that kingdom. They eagerly awaited its restoration. And Jesus announced its imminent restoration.

The story actually begins in the Book of Genesis, when God gives Adam "dominion" over "all the earth" and all the creatures therein, from fish and birds to cattle and bugs (Gen 1:26). Adam is made in God's "image" and "likeness," which suggests a father-son relationship and a delegation of royal responsibilities. Man and woman are made to serve as firstborn vice-regents of God. When the Psalmist revisits this theme, he discusses the dominion in terms of the kingship that God shared willingly with the first man:

What is man that You are mindful of him,
and the son of man that You should care for him?
You have made him little less than the angels,
and crowned him with glory and honor.
You have given him rule over the works of Your hands,
putting all things under his feet. (Ps 8:4–6)

God "crowned" all humankind in Adam and bestowed "dominion" and "rule" upon the primal couple and their offspring. Ancient peoples would have recognized in the Genesis account the
common behavior of kings, who amassed lands to pass on to their
sons and heirs.

But Adam was more than merely a king. He was a *priestly* king.
Genesis relates that God placed him with specific duties, indicated
by the Hebrew verbs *abodah* and *shamar* (usually translated as "to
till" and "to keep"). Elsewhere in the Pentateuch, these verbs appear together only to describe the ritual service of the priests and
Levites in the sanctuary (see Nm 3:7–8, 8:26, 18:5–6). In describing priestly service, they might be rendered "to minister" and "to
guard." The priests were to offer the sacrificial service to God, and
they were to protect His sanctuary from defilement. These literary
clues suggest the biblical authors' intent to describe all creation as
a royal temple built by a heavenly king. Adam is intentionally portrayed as a royal firstborn and high-priestly figure, a priest-king set
to rule as vice-regent over the temple-kingdom of creation.

God seals all this in a special way. The terms of man's relationship with God are ordered by the covenant of the Sabbath established on the seventh day. The Hebrew word for a covenant oath is
sheva, which means seven. To swear is, literally, to "seven oneself."
Covenant, then, is the meaning of God's Sabbath rest. It could not

have been for God's respite, since the Almighty does not grow weary. No, God is here creating a covenant bond—that is, a *family* bond—with the cosmos. By breathing life into Adam, He bestowed His Spirit of sonship upon the man. Adam was to rule over the world as a *son of God.* This view is borne out not only in the teaching of the Catholic Church, but also in the writings of the ancient rabbis. Modern scholars have referred to God's seventh-day blessing as the "Cosmic Covenant."

In the story of creation, we see God amassing a realm and then establishing humankind as His royal family on earth. He solemnly seals his decree by establishing an everlasting covenant.

This covenant is key to understanding the Book of Genesis—and the entire Bible, which itself is divided into the "Old Covenant" and the "New Covenant." (The Hebrew word for covenant, *b'rith,* and the Greek, *diatheke,* are usually translated into English as "testament.") When we take Genesis on its own terms, it is intelligible. When we try to impose our terms on the text, however, the text disintegrates before our eyes.

Some people, for example, read Genesis as an ancient science textbook, and so they find it wanting. But it was not written as a science textbook. It is, on one level, a charter of kingship—the kingship of Adam, whose name means both "a man" and "humankind." One of the terms of God's covenant with the human race was dominion: Adam and Eve were to fill the earth and subdue it. Thus, God made the cosmos for their good and for their delight. He made the cosmos knowable for them in a way it was not knowable to the other animals. Our knowledge of creation differs from theirs not only in degree, but in kind. The human mind, then, was conformed to creation; and creation was made for the human mind. This is the cosmic anthropic principle in its primal form.

And this term of the covenant, this charter of dominion and king-ship—along with the necessary intelligibility of creation—is what made the natural sciences and technologies possible.

In giving the world to Adam, God gave the human race a king-dom to rule as His vicars. By their pride and disobedience, how-ever, Adam and Eve forfeited their privileged status. When the serpent tempted them, they renounced their divinely appointed offices. Adam failed to protect the garden sanctuary from the deadly intruder; and, by taking the forbidden fruit, he and Eve re-fused to make a sacrifice of their desire for earthly goods. They refused, too, to exercise dominion over the beast that confronted them. Thus Adam failed in both his royal and priestly tasks. He abdicated the kingship God had shared with him, and in doing so he bequeathed the heritage of his failure to all generations in his line.

This, the Original Sin, is a disaster of cosmic proportions. Yet the ancient Christians, and their modern descendants, could sing of the fall from grace as a "happy fault"—because it created the need for a savior, the actual occasion of the incarnation of the eter-nal Word of God. From the wreckage of the fall, God would ac-complish a still greater work for humanity. Because of Adam's self-destruction, the world would await a restoration.

THE COMEBACK TRAIL

But salvation was a long way off. In the subsequent chapters of Genesis, the human family grows more rebellious, beginning with Cain's murder of his brother Abel and continuing through the worldwide decadence at the time of Noah. God partially re-establishes cosmic order by saving the family of Noah; but sin once again appears on the scene. With the arrogant self-worship at the

Tower of Babel, the human family is once again dispersed, exiled from God and even from one another. These evil generations have wandered far from humanity's original kingly vocation.

Yet then comes Abraham, a man of faith, to whom God promises a future restoration of the cosmic covenant. To Abraham and his descendants, God promises divine blessing for all the families of the earth (Gen 12:3); a fruitful land (12:1); and a line of kings (17:6). And God seals each of these promises with a covenant (see Gen 15, 17:4–8, and 22:15–18), thus re-establishing the bonds of kinship between God and a human family. It is through Abraham that we also glimpse a priest-king, Melchizedek, king of Salem (Gen 14:18), who blesses Abraham as he offers a sacrifice of bread and wine to God. (Salem will later be renamed Jeru-salem and identified with Mount Zion; see Ps 76:2.) God's covenant with Abraham marks a partial restoration, a partial fulfillment that would one day be complete, universal, cosmic—catholic.

But only after further setbacks. For, within just a few generations, God's family would again sin grievously, this time bringing upon themselves the punishment of slavery in a foreign land. But this, too, proves to be a "fortunate fault," as slavery in Egypt provides the occasion of God's great saving work of the Exodus. The biblical narrative describing Israel's liberation everywhere echoes the Genesis narrative of creation. Israel is delivered through water as a new creation. The cloud of divine presence covers Mount Sinai for six days before God calls Moses, on the seventh day, to enter the cloud and receive the blueprint for God's dwelling (Ex 24). God's instructions appear in sevens, again like His work of creation, and His seven commands conclude with ordinances for observance of the seventh day, the Sabbath. The making of the priestly vestments and the building of the tabernacle recall the creation narrative. In both, the work proceeds through seven stages (which, in Exodus, conclude with "as the Lord commanded Moses"). Moses beholds his handiwork, as God did in Genesis, and blesses it (Ex 39:43). As God "finished His work," so Moses "finished the work" (Gen 2:1–2; Ex 40:34). And as God rested on the seventh day, blessing and hallowing it, so when Moses finished his work, the divine presence filled the tabernacle (Ex 40:34).

With the Exodus, God restored a royal priesthood, a priestly kingship. He declared Israel to be His "own possession among all peoples ... a kingdom of priests and a holy nation" (Ex 19:5–6). He set them in the place of Adam, the priest-king. What Adam was to be for every person, Israel was to be for every nation—a royal priest, "the firstborn of many brethren" (see Rom 8:29). As Adam had been made in God's image and likeness, so God addressed Israel with titles suggesting royal-priestly primogeniture. To Him, Israel is "My son, My firstborn (Ex 4:22–23, 19:6).

Nevertheless, just as the Israelites received Adam's vocation, they also perpetrated an Adam-like fall from grace. And just as the original fall had resulted in exile and de-consecration of the royal-priestly figure, so too did Israel's idolatrous worship of the golden calf. God disinherited His people, pointedly telling Moses that they are "*your* people, whom *you* brought out of the land of Egypt" (Ex 32:7). In defiling itself through ritual rebellion, Israel, like Adam, had become unfit for the divine vocation. And never again does the Old Testament use the royal-priestly title of Exodus 19:6 to describe the people of Israel.

Still, on the strength of His covenant with their father Abraham (see Ex 32:13), God spared Israel and permitted the tribes, eventually, to enter the promised land. So God's people experienced, again, a partial restoration.

In the promised land, Israel remained a people set apart. A nation unlike any other, they were governed not by human laws, but by God Himself through His prophets. Yet they were inexorably drawn to the trappings of kingship, which they saw in the neighboring pagan lands. They wanted power, prestige, loot, and conquest. In other words, they no longer wished to be a nation set apart. They longed to be like everyone else. They demanded that the prophet Samuel appoint a king for them (see 1 Sam 8). Like Adam's sin in Eden and Israel's in Sinai, this petition marked a rebellion against God's rule. Moses had foreseen this day; and so, grudgingly, in the Book of Deuteronomy he had provided laws to govern the behavior of Israel's kings.

Samuel told the people what they could expect from a king: taxes, military conscription, and oppression. But the people insisted, and God let them have their way. Samuel ritually installed Saul in his kingly office by anointing, an action formerly used only for the ordination of priests. As soon as he was anointed, Saul began to prophesy. Thus, God showed His people that, even though they had rejected His rule, He could continue to rule them through their king. They hadn't chosen Saul as their king; *God* had chosen him as their king. Thus, even though Saul was a proud and arrogant man, as king he was "the anointed," which in Hebrew is *messiah* and in Greek *christos*, whence we get the English title "Christ." Though Saul's misdeeds would eventually bring down his reign and his dynasty, they could not bring down the validity of the kingship God had established.

Ultimately, God would turn Israel's demand for a king, like all of mankind's previous rebellions, into the occasion for an even greater work on His part. From the ruins of Saul's reign arose an even greater royal house—an even greater messiah-king—indeed, a blessing for Israel and, through Israel, for all the nations.

Thus, in spite of mankind's repeated failure to live up to its royal-priestly vocation, the restoration of the cosmic covenant proceeded in history at the pace of God's providence. God first gathered into one kingdom all the sons of Abraham, so that He might eventually gather all the sons of Adam.

Twelve

THE FLEETING AND FUTURE KINGDOM

The Difference David Made

As psalmist, monarch, and ancestor of Jesus Christ—and as a man after God's own heart (1 Sam 13:14)—King David amounts to so much more than we would guess from popular homiletics. Don't get me wrong: I'm not saying that no one preaches or writes about David. Such a charge would be absurd. David stars in the Bible's emblematic tale of repentance, the aftermath of his dalliance with Bathsheba. As such, he's a stock figure in sermons of every denomination.

But David is so much more than that. Within the Bible, he is the man who defines kingship—a kingship that had merely been suggested in the stories of the creation and the Exodus. He establishes the only lasting royal house in the Old Testament, and the longest-running dynasty in the ancient world.

Scholars and preachers usually acknowledge David as the dominating figure in the Book of Psalms, with more than seventy psalms attributed to him. What is not widely recognized is his prominence throughout the Old Testament. Without a doubt, the lively memory of David and his kingdom are central to the Gospel of Jesus

Christ; but it is perhaps even more important to the direction and meaning of the Old Testament.

Why has David been relatively neglected? It's hard to say. But one reason is that researchers have tended to focus instead on the importance and influence of Moses and the covenant at Sinai.

Moses is indeed a gigantic figure of influence in both Testaments of the Bible. But is David any less? Consider just a few points. While the name *Moses* occurs more than 720 times in the Old Testament, *David* is mentioned almost 1,020 times. David's career is the subject of forty-two chapters, or nearly 30 percent, of what ancient rabbis call the "Former Prophets" (Joshua–2 Kings). In Chronicles, a review of Israel's history from a priestly perspective, the percentage is even greater.

In the prophets, David is mentioned thirty-seven times, and Moses only seven. And the hopes of the Jewish people usually find their focus in Mount Zion, the site of David's royal palace, rather than Sinai, where Moses received the Law. Even today, the Jewish movement to re-establish the ancient homeland is known as "Zionism," and its symbol belongs not to the Lawgiver but to the King: the Star of David.

When the ancient Israelites, and later the Jews, spoke of "the kingdom," the reign of David provided their only historical referent. If the stories of Adam, Abraham, and Moses foretold the reign of a priestly king, that priestly king was David—and, in turn, his house, his line, his "son."

House of the Rising Sun

Scripture tells us that David was a man after God's own heart (1 Sam 13:14). He was indeed a man *unlike* Saul. While Saul looked princely, David was a mere youth, small in stature (1 Sam 16:7).

But when "Samuel took the horn of oil and anointed him in the midst of his brothers... the Spirit of the Lord came mightily upon David from that day forward" (I Sam 16:13).

At the same time, the Lord withdrew His Spirit from Saul, who was then tormented by demons. The demons relented only when David played his lyre. (Similarly, the demons would one day run from Jesus, confessing Him to be the anointed, the Christ. See Luke 4:41.)

Saul brought about his own demise when he opposed God's will and sought to kill David. As David assumed the throne, he began a reign quite unlike Saul's. He moved the nation's capital to Jerusalem, in order to unite the tribes. Once David had firmly established himself at Jerusalem, he decided to bring the Ark of the Covenant there—the shrine that contained the Law God gave to Israel, along with other relics, such as Aaron's priestly staff and manna from heaven. The presence of the Ark would make Jerusalem not just the political center of Israel, but the religious center as well. David himself led the procession that carried the Ark to its destination. The king was dressed not in royal robes, but in priestly vestments: a linen ephod. He danced for joy "with all his might" before the Ark. And when the procession had reached its new home, David himself offered the sacrifices.

Why was it all right for David to act as a priest? He was not, after all, a member of the tribe of Levi. When Saul, earlier, had tried offering sacrifices, he was severely punished. But there was a huge difference between David and Saul. Saul's sacrifices were just a business transaction with God. But David danced and made offerings out of love and joy—not because he wanted something from God.

David was a priestly king, as God had intended Adam to be. He possessed a royal priesthood, as God had intended Israel to hold.

David and his son, Solomon, were to be, like Melchizedek, priest-kings who reigned and offered sacrifice in (Jeru)Salem (see Ps 110:1–4).

Yet David was not satisfied. He desired something more: he wanted to build a Temple for God in Jerusalem. So he consulted with the prophet Nathan: "See now, I dwell in a house of cedar, but the ark of God dwells in a tent" (2 Sam 7:2). God, however, did not intend for David to build the Temple. God had something much more important in store for his king. Nathan spoke God's word to David:

> The Lord declares to you that the Lord will make you a
> house ... I will establish the throne of his kingdom for ever.
> I will be his father, and he shall be My son. When he
> commits iniquity, I will chasten him with the rod of men,
> with the stripes of the sons of men; but I will not take My
> steadfast love from him, as I took it from Saul, whom I put
> away from before you. And your house and your kingdom
> shall be made sure forever before Me; your throne shall be
> established for ever. (2 Sam 7:11–16)

God here renewed His *covenant* with Israel through the house of David. He re-established His family bond with His people, using the language of close kinship. As Adam and then Israel would live as God's "firstborn," so David's heir would enjoy a father-son relationship with the Almighty. This time, however, it came with an everlasting guarantee.

The terms of the covenant are rather remarkable:

- *The Lord will make you a house:* David will be not just king for a day or a lifetime, but the founder of a royal dynasty.

- *I will establish his kingdom:* The son of David will be ruler of a vast kingdom that includes all of Israel, but also the rest of the world, "the nations" (see Ps 2:8; 72:11, 16). The Books of Chronicles go so far as to call it the "Kingdom of Yahweh" (see 1 Chr 28:5; 2 Chr 13:8).
- *He shall build a house for My name:* David's son will build the temple as a permanent home for the Ark of the Covenant.
- *I will be his father, and he shall be My son:* David's son would be adopted as God's own son. This is the first time divine sonship is explicitly applied to one individual. Before this, the whole people of Israel had been called God's firstborn son (Ex 4:22), but no single person had ever been "son of God."
- *I will chasten him . . . but I will not take My steadfast love from him:* God would never disown David's line the way He disowned Saul, no matter how much his descendants might sin. The covenant would be permanent. Like a loving father, God would punish His son, but only for his own good.
- *Your throne shall be established for ever:* The dynasty of David would never end. Dynasties rise and fall in all other earthly monarchies, but the throne of David would always be occupied by a descendant of David himself.

KEYS OF DAVID

Since David's kingdom would be everlasting, it would come to define "kingdom" for all subsequent generations raised on the word of God. It was not merely a theoretical concept or theological metaphor. It had a definite historical shape, vividly and specifically recorded by Israel's historians, prophets, and poets. And the qualities they record relate directly to the terms of the covenant revealed by the prophet Nathan.

What did David's kingdom look like? It's important that we know, because—as Jesus Himself made clear—the contours of "the kingdom" mark the shape of our salvation. The heart of Jesus' earthly ministry was the proclamation of the kingdom, and His use of that word could mean only one thing to His hearers. They understood Him to mean the restoration of the kingdom of David, and He did not contradict their expectation. In fact, He confirmed it and clarified it, never diminishing its Davidic character.

From the historical sources, we can identify certain elements that prevailed as long as the House of David ruled from Jerusalem. Here I would like to identify seven primary features of God's covenant with the House of David and three secondary features. I focus on these ten because they are integral to the dynastic drama we read in the later books of the Old Testament, and also because they will re-emerge as keys to the Davidic identity of Jesus Christ—and the Church He established on earth.

1. *The Davidic monarchy was founded upon a divine covenant*, the only human kingdom of the Old Testament to enjoy such a privilege (see 2 Sam 8:11–16).

2. *The Davidic monarch was the Son of God.* The familial relationship of the king to God is expressed in Nathan's oracle, but again in other places (see Psalm 2:7). The son of David received the grace of divine sonship at the time of his anointing.

3. *The son of David was "the Christ,"* that is, "the messiah," since *mashiach* in Hebrew literally means "the anointed one" (see I Sam 16:13; I Kgs 1:43–48; 2 Kgs 11:12; Ps 89:20–39). His anointing with oil made him a priest and a king, "a priest forever after the order of Melchizedek" (Ps 110:4). Melchizedek

was priest-king in the Jerusalem of Abraham's time (Gen 14:18; Ps 76:2).

4. *The House of David was inextricably bound to Jerusalem, particularly Mount Zion,* which was the personal possession of King David and his heirs (2 Sam 5:9). More than the capital city for the monarchy, Jerusalem became the spiritual center of God's people, and the place of pilgrimage for Israel and all the nations (Is 2:1–3).

5. *The Temple was the visible sign of the Davidic covenant and God's kingdom.* Building the Temple was central to the terms of the covenant, and the same Hebrew word for "house" was used to describe not only David's dynasty, but also God's dwelling place, which was to serve as a "house of prayer for all peoples" (Is 56:7; Mt 21:12–15).

6. *The Davidic King was to rule over all twelve tribes of Israel—but also over all the nations.* It was only under David and Solomon that both Judah and all the northern tribes were united as one kingdom and freed from foreign oppression (see 2 Sam 5:1–5; I Kgs 4:1–19). The Lord also decreed that the Davidic king was to rule over all the nations (Ps 2:8, 72:1–17), and welcome gentile pilgrims to Jerusalem (I Kgs 8:41–43, 10:1–24), from all over the world. The Davidic Kingdom at *Zion* thus marks the first time Israel was called to welcome gentiles as an integral part of their covenant with God.

7. *The monarchy was to be everlasting.* One of the most prevalent emphases in the Psalms and histories is that David's dynasty will be eternal (see 2 Sam 7:16). Not only the dynasty, but also the life

span of the reigning monarch was described as everlasting (see Ps 21:4).

Along with those seven primary features, we should note three secondary elements. Though these were not mentioned explicitly in Nathan's oracle, they are found throughout the histories and hymns of the House of David. Again, they will become even more important under the New Covenant of Jesus Christ.

1. The *Queen Mother* became an important part of the royal government. It starts with King Solomon in I Kings 2:19:

> So Bathsheba went to King Solomon, to speak to him on behalf of Adonijah. And the king rose to meet her, and bowed down to her; then he sat on his throne, and had a seat brought for the king's mother; and she sat on his right.

Note, here, that everyone bowed before Solomon, but Solomon himself bowed down before his mother. From that point on, the Queen Mother became a permanent fixture in the kingdom, a symbol of the continuity of David's royal line. She also served as one of the king's most important advisers. Indeed, Proverbs 31 is identified as the advice of the queen mother of King Lemuel: "The words of Lemuel, king of Massa, which his mother taught him." When the prophet Jeremiah addresses the king, he addresses his mother as well, such was her authority: "Say to the king and the queen-mother . . ." (Jer 13:18; see also 2 Kgs 24:15).

2. The *"prime minister"* or chief steward became a distinct office in the royal government. The king had many servants (in I Kgs 4:7

there are twelve), but one man was chief among them and stood between the king and his other ministers. Almost two centuries after David, Isaiah prophesied a transition in the royal government in which one prime minister would be replaced by another (see Is 22:15–25). From his prophecy, we can tell that everyone in the kingdom could identify the prime minister: "he shall be a father to the inhabitants of Jerusalem and to the house of Judah." The sign of the prime minister's office was the *keys of the kingdom.* "And I will place on his shoulder the key of the house of David; he shall open, and none shall shut; and he shall shut, and none shall open."

3. *The thank offering* or "sacrifice of thanksgiving" became the primary liturgy celebrated at Temple, much more than the sin offering (see Ps 50:13–14, 116:17–19). The thank offering (Lev 7:12–15) included unleavened bread and wine freely offered to God in gratitude for deliverance. Ancient Jewish teachers predicted that, when the Messiah came, no other sacrifice would be offered: the thank offering alone would continue. The word for "thank offering" is *todah* in Hebrew, but is translated as *eucharistia* in many Greek translations of the Scriptures and in the writings of ancient Jews, such as Philo and Aquila.

THRONE AWAY

Under David, and then under his son Solomon, the kingdom flourished. God delivered on His promise of peace, stability, and a family bond between Himself and His people. The blessings of the covenant seemed evident everywhere, and the foreign nations all wanted a piece of it. They sought to make alliances with Solomon. They sent delegations to Jerusalem to pay homage to Solomon's

God. And Solomon designed his Temple to accommodate the worship of the gentiles, as "a house of prayer for all nations" (Is 56:7). So great was the prestige and prosperity of Israel that the memory of those generations—of David and Solomon—would remain indelible, especially for the tribe of Judah, for millennia afterward.

Yet the historical reality of the kingdom fell apart, very quickly.

Like Adam before him, like Israel before him, Solomon sinned grievously and then fell into a downward spiral of sin. He flouted the laws of Moses that governed his kingship; he overtaxed the tribes and mulitiplied wives for himself (seven hundred!) and concubines (three hundred!). These sins led to still deadlier sins. The Scriptures tell us that "his wives turned his heart . . . to strange gods" (I Kgs 11:1–3). Once the archetypal wise man, Solomon now became an idolater.

When Solomon died, his son Rehoboam refused to renegotiate the kingdom's taxation policies, and the tribes rebelled. Ten of the twelve tribes split off and established a Northern Kingdom—separating themselves not only from the kingdom of David, but also from the worship of the Temple. All that was left for the House of David were the two tiny tribes of Judah and Benjamin.

In this period of decay, great prophets arose to herald a revival of the House of David. Isaiah prophesied that salvation would come with the birth of an heir to David's throne. The new king's dominion would be vast and would endure "both now and forever" (see Is 9:5–6). Elsewhere (see Is 11:1–16), Isaiah predicted the sprouting of a new shoot from the root of Jesse, who was the father of David. The prophets repeatedly portrayed the restoration as a recapitulation of God's covenants of the past; it would be like a new creation, a new exodus, as well as a new kingdom.

The prophets, however, could not halt Israel's decline. Badly weakened, the divided kingdom was easy prey for its neighbors—

the lands that had once been eager to win the favor of Jerusalem's king. The Northern Kingdom was destroyed in 722 B.C., overrun by the Assyrians. In 597, Babylon sacked Jerusalem, shattering the Southern Kingdom and sending its elites into exile. The conquering king rounded up the descendants of King David, and he mercilessly slaughtered them.

Within a generation after David's death, the "everlasting kingdom" had vanished. Within five hundred years the royal lineage, too, was apparently extinguished.

So much had seemed near at hand: the fulfillment of God's promise to Abraham, to bless all peoples through Abraham's seed; the rehabilitation of Israel as a priestly nation through the sacrifice of the Temple; and even the restoration of God's cosmic covenant with all the children of Adam.

HOPE SPRINGS ETERNAL

Still, the words of the prophets held out the promise, and history recorded God's oracle through Nathan as an unconditional surety.

In the second half of the sixth century B.C., after Babylon fell to Persia, some Israelites returned to Jerusalem and began to rebuild the Temple. The Second Temple was just a shadow of Solomon's, a humiliating reminder of how far the land and people had fallen, from prosperity and from God.

The literature between the testaments records the residual hope that the House of David would be restored: "raise up unto them their king, the son of David . . . that he may reign over Israel Your servant . . . For all shall be holy and their king the anointed [*Messiah, Christ*] of the Lord!" The Dead Sea Scrolls witness to the same hope: "He is the branch of David who shall arise . . . in Zion at the end of time. As it is written, 'I will raise up the tent of David that is fallen.' That is to say, the fallen tent of David is he who shall arise to save Israel."

The hope endured, in spite of the apparent impossibility of its fulfillment. The tent of David, after all, had fallen. The tree of Jesse had been cut down. But it was God who had made His covenant with the House of David, God who had made the promises. Almighty, He could raise up children of Abraham from stones if He willed. He could draw up a branch of David from the stump of the family tree.

He who made the covenant had also created the earth, and He could gather the children of Adam once again from the ends of the earth to receive their blessing from the son of David, the son of Abraham.

The idea of a *catholic* faith, a universal faith—willed from creation, promised to Abraham, mediated by Israel, glimpsed in David—remained as the special possession of Israel's remnant. The gentile nations were content with their local gods. But God's people awaited the day of a great king over Israel and the nations. "And I will set up over them one shepherd, My servant David, and he shall feed them: he shall feed them and be their shepherd . . . My servant David shall be king over them; and they shall all have one shepherd. They shall follow My ordinances and be careful to observe My statutes" (Ezk 34:23, 37:24).

Thirteen

THE KINGDOM COME

On Christ the King, the Son of David

There is ample evidence that, in the century before the birth of Christ, God's people sensed—and hoped—that the time was at hand. The time had arrived.

The Septuagint Greek translation of the Old Testament—which was very popular among the Jews who were dispersed in Gentile lands—sometimes added royal titles where none had existed in the Hebrew. In Genesis 49:10, for example, the Septuagint adds that the coming "ruler" will be a "prince."

In the apocryphal book Second Esdras, the divine oracle anticipates the arrival of "My son the Messiah" (2 Esd 7:28–29), who will rule "all people" from "the top of Mount Zion" (13:36–37). Similar language appears in the literature attributed to the Enoch tradition and in the Dead Sea Scrolls. The authors of the latter expected the imminent arrival of not one messiah, but *two*: a kingly warrior and priestly prophet. The Scrolls refer to the future king as both "messiah" and "the branch of David." We find the spirit of the age vividly preserved in the annals of the Jewish historian Josephus, who records the rise and fall of several self-proclaimed messiahs. Josephus himself advanced an improbable candidate for the title: his patron, the Roman emperor Vespasian.

Those who kept the faith lived in hope. Nevertheless, it must have been difficult. The current conditions of God's people were certainly humiliating. The gentiles often mocked the Jews for the stark contrast between their elitism—they claimed to be God's "chosen people"—and their actual status as a vassal state of decadent pagan empires.

For God had clearly spelled out His promises in the covenant with David. David's line would be everlasting. Yet now it seemed to be extinguished. David's son would rule all nations. Yet now the nations were taking turns ruling Israel! The Hebrew Scriptures proclaimed the permanence and majesty of the House of David; but that majesty was nowhere to be found. In fact, the House of David was nowhere to be found.

The situation invited ridicule. The evidence of failure was everywhere. Except for a brief space in the Maccabean period, Israel—or rather, what was left of Israel—was ruled by foreign powers.

FALSE STARTS

Then, after the Maccabean period came a strange interlude, when kings arose who seemed eager and able to restore the fortunes of Israel—*in the very terms of God's covenant with David*. They reconquered almost all the lands that had formerly belonged to Israel, and they forced the male inhabitants to undergo circumcision.

In time there came a king named Herod; historians would refer to him as Herod the Great. He tried mightily to make himself look like the "son of David." He rebuilt the Jerusalem Temple on a grand scale, outdoing even Solomon—and he acquired many wives for himself, just as Solomon had. And the people prospered. Herod's Roman patrons brought some measure of peace, stability, and security to the region.

Herod, however, was not a Jew. Though he kept kosher and made a show of some religious practices, he was born an Edomite, a gentile. Moreover, he was, by all accounts, insane. He brutally murdered three of his own sons, because he feared they would plot his overthrow. This curious combination of outward religiosity and extreme cruelty moved Caesar Augustus to say that he'd rather be Herod's pig than Herod's son. Herod's paranoid spells often ended in murderous purges of his subjects. Once he had hundreds of suspected conspirators crucified along a busy highway, and he left their bodies there to rot for weeks.

Yet Herod's successes were indisputable—the restoration of the land, the recovery of the tribes that had long since mingled with the pagans, and the reconstruction of the Temple. Some people wondered whether he might indeed be the Son of David. After all, even Solomon had his flaws . . .

Herod probably knew better, but his life depended upon the ruse. It is quite possible that he, too, expected a true "son of David" to arrive at any moment. And where would that leave Herod?

Such was the social, political, religious, and covenantal climate at the moment when the Word became flesh, in the moment when He made His dwelling with His people.

A KING IS BORN

"Thus says the Lord: If you can break my covenant with day, and my covenant with night, so that day and night no longer alternate in sequence, then can my covenant with my servant David also be broken" (Jer 33:19–21). Thus said the Lord through the Prophet Jeremiah—*after* the kingdom of David's descendants had already fallen down in a heap.

And those who had faith continued in hope. God had made very specific promises to King David. They could not be any clearer, even if circumstances had made the promises seem absurd. The prayer of God's people in the Old Testament continued to rise heavenward during the reign of Herod: "How long, O Lord?"

We see the answer to the question—and the answer to the prayers—in the very first words of the New Testament: "The book of the genealogy of Jesus Christ, the son of David, the son of Abraham" (Mt 1:1). Addressing a Jewish readership, Matthew identifies Jesus as "the Christ," the anointed, the awaited Messiah. He adds that, true to expectations, the Messiah is born into the House of David and from the stock of Abraham. By invoking those two names, Matthew evoked the covenants. Thus, from the beginning of his Gospel, he makes clear that he is announcing the arrival of the *kingdom*. That is the essence of his "good news" (the literal meaning of the word "Gospel"). The covenants had been fulfilled. The promised kingdom had come, and it was indeed a universal kingdom, consisting of both Israel and the gentiles. "Kings shall come forth from you . . . Abraham shall become a great and mighty nation, and all the nations of the earth shall bless themselves by him" (Gen 17:6, 18:18). "I will establish the throne of [David's] kingdom for ever" (2 Sam 7:13–14).

The long-awaited king had come, the son of David, the son of God, the Christ—the anointed. And He had the royal pedigree to prove it.

Matthew's genealogy begins with Abraham, but it centers on the kingdom of David. The four fixed points are the life of Abraham, the reign of David, the fall of the house of David at the Babylon-

ian exile, and the arrival of Jesus. Matthew compresses the generations so that they fall into three groups of fourteen—the numeral
that, in Hebrew, spells out the name David (*DVD*). In Hebrew, as
in Latin, letters stand for numbers; so the genealogy of the son of
David repeatedly reinforces its identity with the royal family.

As his narrative unfolds, Matthew shows us the convergence of
the two contenders for the kingship: Herod and Jesus. Jesus is born
in Bethlehem, the city of David, which the prophets had identified
as the birthplace of the Messiah-king (Mt 2:6; Mic 5:2). Moreover, He is born of a virgin, thus fulfilling Isaiah's prophecy of the
Davidic king: "Behold, a virgin shall conceive and bear a son" (Mt
1:23; Is 7:14).

At Jesus' birth, the gentiles, represented by the Magi, come to
pay tribute to the newborn king, just as they did to the original son
of David, King Solomon (Ps 72:10–11). The Magi find Jesus with
Mary—the king with his queen mother, as they would have encountered Solomon with Bathsheba in the long-ago royal court of
Jerusalem (see 1 Kgs 2:19).

The appearance of the Magi provokes one of Herod's murderous rages, and so he orders the massacre of the innocents. The holy
family must flee the country, just as the legitimately anointed
David had been forced to flee from the envious wrath of the divinely deposed Saul.

THE KING'S SELF-DISCLOSURE

It is not just the evangelists who identify Jesus as king and the kingdom as Davidic. It is not just a matter of imposing prophecies on
the scenes. Repeatedly, bystanders and even his enemies give Jesus
the title. Consider the blind men who cry out "Have mercy on us,
son of David!" (Mt 9:27, 20:30) or the Canaanite woman who

seeks a healing for her daughter (Mt 15:22). The crowd that wel-
comes Jesus to David's capital, Jerusalem, greets him with "Hosanna
to the son of David!" (Mt 21:9). The hostile Pharisees identify
"the Christ" with "the son of David" (Mt 22:42). Even Pilate and
the Roman soldiers mock Jesus with Davidic titles (Mt 27:11, 29,
37), and the crowd jeeringly confirms that the son of David should
also be the son of God (Mt 27:40).

Jesus does not refuse or deny the Davidic titles, but rather confirms them with His own pronouncements. One chapter begins
with the story of Jesus and His disciples picking grain on the Sabbath, an action that Jesus justifies by comparing Himself and His
men with David and his band: "Have you not read what David did,
when he was hungry . . . ?" (Mt 12:3). Later in the same chapter,
the people ask one another: "Can this be the Son of David?"
(12:23). Jesus responds to them by saying, "If it is by the Spirit of
God that I cast out demons, then the kingdom of God has come
upon you" (12:28).

The Gospels clearly identify Jesus as "son of God" and as "son
of David," as a king and as the anointed. His kingdom is clearly the
kingdom of God, but also the kingdom of David. This is confirmed in the small details. For the reign of Jesus, as we find it in
the Gospels, displays the consistent characteristics of the Davidic
monarchy. Let's revisit those seven primary and three secondary
features of God's covenant with David, and let's see how well Jesus
fills the role.

I. *The Davidic monarchy was founded upon a divine covenant.* God's
   covenant with David, as described in Nathan's oracle (2 Sam
   7:9–16), provides all the content of the angelic description of
   Jesus in Luke 1:32–33. Later, Jesus associates His kingship with
   a "new covenant" (Lk 22:20) and states that a kingdom has

been assigned (literally, "covenanted") to Him by the Father (Lk 22:29).

2. *The Davidic monarch was the Son of God.* Jesus is the natural, not merely adopted, Son of God (Lk 1:35), and the title is used of Him throughout the New Testament.

3. *The son of David was "the Christ."* "Christ" is indeed the preferred title of Jesus, from the first line of the New Testament onward. Indeed, He is the "Lord's Christ" (Lk 2:26), a title applied only to kings in the Old Testament (see I Sam 16:6).

4. *The House of David was inextricably bound to Jerusalem.* The climactic scenes of Jesus' ministry occur in Jerusalem—His trial, passion, and death. The Gospel makes it clear that the word of God should go forth "from Jerusalem" to the ends of the earth (Lk 24:47).

5. *The monarchy was also bound to the Temple.* Luke's Gospel begins in the Temple. Jesus' childhood is set there. Jesus cleanses the Temple and evicts the moneychangers. For most of the Gospel he is traveling there (9:51–19:27), and the climax is reached when Jesus arrives in Jerusalem, where he cleanses—and teaches within—the Temple (Lk 19:45–21:38).

6. *The Davidic king is destined to rule all twelve tribes of Israel—but also all the nations.* The Gospels show—by many signs—that Jesus intends to restore the unity of the twelve tribes. He appoints twelve Apostles, and He promises that they will judge "the twelve tribes of Israel" (Lk 22:30). Key figures, such as the prophetess Anna, from the tribe of Asher, represent a faithful remnant from the

"lost" northern tribes (Lk 2:36). And Jesus gained a "muliti-tude" (Lk 19:37) of followers from the former lands of united Israel by preaching in Galilee, Samaria, and Judea. By His entry into Jerusalem, he has formed a reunited kingdom. Yet Jesus' kingship extends over all the nations. Simeon announces that He will be a "light of revelation to the nations" (Lk 2:32). Luke traces genealogy back to Adam rather than Abraham. Jesus heals gentiles as well as Jews (e.g., Lk 7:1–10). He predicts that "men will come from east and west, and from north and south" to sit at table in the kingdom of God (Lk 13:29). He commands that "forgiveness of sins should be preached in His name to *all nations*, beginning from Jerusalem" (Lk 24:47).

7. *The kingdom of David was to be everlasting.* The angel Gabriel prom-ises Mary that Jesus "will reign over the house of Jacob forever, and of His kingdom there will be no end" (Lk 1:33).

The three secondary characteristics find fulfillment in the Gospel as well.

1. Mary appears as *Queen Mother* when she advises her royal son (Jn 2:3), when she pleads the cause of His subjects, when she re-ceives foreign dignitaries with Him (Mt 2:11), and when she stands with His court of twelve royal ministers, the Apostles (Jn 19:25; Acts 2:14).

2. Jesus appoints Peter as prime minister using the very terms used in the appointment of the "steward" who governs "the house-hold of David" as vice-regent (see Mt 16:19; Is 22:15–25). The king bestows authority symbolically with "the keys." (We'll come back to this yet again.)

3. Jesus renews the sacrifice of Thanksgiving, the *todah*, by His own offering of bread and wine, the *eucharistia*, the Eucharist. Indeed, whenever we find Jesus breaking bread, we see Him "giving thanks" (e.g., Lk 24:30–35; Jn 6:11).

No one who believes the Gospels can deny that Jesus' contemporaries awaited a Messiah-king from the House of David. No one who believes the Gospels can deny that Jesus presented Himself as the awaited Davidic king.

If Jesus is the Davidic king, His kingdom must be, in some sense, a Davidic kingdom—*the* Davidic kingdom. Jesus' "kingdom of God" did not supplant or replace the everlasting kingdom created by the covenant with David. Jesus' kingdom *was* that kingdom, and *is* that kingdom, brought to fulfillment.

For only David's kingdom was called the "kingdom of Yahweh" (1 Chr 28:5). The Old Testament authors understood that the reign of the house of David was based on a divine covenant in which the son of David was also declared to be the Son of God (2 Sam 7:14; Ps 2:7). Therefore, the kingdom of David was the manifestation of God's rule over the earth—that is, God's everlasting kingdom for Israel and the nations.

But where is that kingdom today? Indeed, where has it been all the years since Jesus' ascension? For the Christian apologist, ancient or modern, there is perhaps no more important question.

Fourteen

WHEN THE REIGN COMES

The Church Is the Kingdom

The modernist biblical scholar Alfred Loisy prophesied his own loss of faith when he sardonically remarked: "Jesus proclaimed the kingdom; what came was the Church."

But Loisy was not merely speaking for himself. This juxtaposition of Church and kingdom had become a commonplace in certain scholarly circles by the end of the nineteenth century.

When it comes to the kingdom of God, there is indeed often a gap between believers' expectations and the Lord's fulfillment. People with better dispositions than Alfred Loisy have been vexed by the problem. Consider the profound dejection of the disciples after Jesus' death: "But we had hoped that He was the one to redeem Israel" (Lk 24:21).

They had expected their redemption to come with a military reconquest or with a miraculous intervention from heaven. They did not expect redemption to entail suffering, death, and apparent failure. When they prayed for a kingdom, they certainly didn't expect the Church. Yet that's what they got.

Throughout the centuries, Jews have cited Jesus' "failure" to produce the expected kingdom as obvious evidence against Christianity's claims. Pagan opponents to Christianity (Celsus in the second century, Julian in the fourth) took the same line of argument. In the nineteenth and twentieth centuries, however, certain *Christians* joined their voices to this unusual chorus. Alfred Loisy was among them, but he was hardly alone. Another was the German F. C. Baur, who claimed that Paul invented Christianity as we know it today, in order to accommodate the non-appearance of the kingdom.

On the opposite end of the theological spectrum from Baur and Loisy, the American dispensationalist C. I. Scofield—whose famous *Scofield Reference Bible* has nurtured generations of American fundamentalists—attempted a response to liberal critics, but he accepted their claim that there was a breakdown between expectation and fulfillment of the kingdom. Scofield's version went like this: Jesus offered the kingdom to the Jews, but they rejected Him, so He established the Church instead, as a "great parenthesis" between the ministry of Jesus and the coming of the true kingdom, which will not arrive until after the "rapture."

In the days immediately after the resurrection, one disciple asked: "Lord, will you at this time restore the kingdom to Israel?" (Acts 1:6). And the anguished question echoes down the millennia. It's clear that, after all these years, some disciples still find an unbearable disparity between what God promised and what Christians got.

We must ask, however, whether the problem is with God's provision or with human expectations. Turn with me to the moment in Scripture when Jesus proclaimed His kingdom in the clearest and most intimate terms—at the Last Supper. Since Luke's Gospel provides the greatest abundance of kingdom-related details, that's where we'll look most closely.

A Meal Fit for a King

Luke's account of the Last Supper is a key text for linking the identity of Jesus as the royal "son of David" with the Church as the Davidic "kingdom of God." At that table, Jesus established the Apostles as His vice-regents, the men who would thenceforth exercise authority in His name. In the Acts of the Apostles—the book Luke wrote as a sequel to his Gospel—we see the Apostles exercising the authority Jesus had given them, as they rule over the Church.

Luke, more than any other evangelist, associates the imagery of *kingdom* with *table fellowship*. Scholars identify ten separate meals in Luke, all of which may be viewed as foretastes of the Messiah's banquet foretold by the Old Testament prophets (see Is 25:6–8; Zech 8:7–8, 19–23). This is particularly evident in the meals hosted by the Messiah Himself: the feeding of the five thousand (9:10–17), the Last Supper (22:7–38), and the meal at Emmaus (24:13–35). In those three meals in Luke—and in them alone—is bread said to be "broken"; the same expression will be used in Acts 2:42, 46; 20:7, 11; 27:35.

Kingdom motifs distinguish these three meals:

- all five thousand are "satisfied" and twelve baskets full of leftovers (9:17), bespeaking the fullness of the twelve tribes of Israel under the Son of David (see 1 Kgs 4:20, 8:65–66);
- the Last Supper is closely associated with the imminent coming of the kingdom (see Lk 22:16, 18, 29–30);
- and the Emmaus sequence is initiated with the disciples' remark "We had hoped He was the one *to redeem Israel,*" that is, to restore the kingdom of David (see Lk 1:68–69).

In sharing meals, Jesus was acting like His royal ancestor. David had extended covenant loyalty through royal-table fellowship (2 Sam 9:7, 10, 13; I Kgs 2:7). The Psalms of David use images of eating and drinking to celebrate God's provision, and the prophets describe the restoration of David's city (Is 25:6–8; Jer 31:12–14) and David's covenant (Is 55:1–5) with images of feasting. In Ezekiel the primary role of the Davidic "shepherd" is to "feed" Israel (Ezk 34:23).

So it is in true kingly character that Jesus says to His Apostles: "I have earnestly desired to eat this passover with you before I suffer; for I tell you I shall not eat it until it is fulfilled in the kingdom of God." Then He took a cup, and when He had given thanks, He said, "Take this, and divide it among yourselves; for I tell you that from now on I shall not drink of the fruit of the vine until the kingdom of God comes" (Lk 22:15–18).

Jesus emphasizes here that the Supper is somehow related to the kingdom and its arrival, and indeed that the kingdom is coming now. He associates the kingdom with eating and drinking, as He does again a few verses later, when He assures the disciples that they will "eat and drink . . . in My kingdom" (v. 30). Those two statements frame the Supper story, and they make a promise: eating and drinking with Jesus will be important manifestations of the kingdom's presence. A few days later, when the risen Christ eats with the disciples, those moments provide His guarantee that the kingdom was truly present.

Breaking News

If Jesus' promise is the frame of the story, the focal point is the so-called "narrative of institution." The words of institution are certainly strange, though Christians have become inured to them over the millennia. Jesus, the king and the anointed, identifies Himself with the broken bread and the wine: "This is My body . . . this cup . . . is the new covenant in My blood" (Lk 22:19–20). Then, in Luke's and Paul's telling of the story, we hear Jesus' command to repeat this meal "in remembrance" of Him. It is this command that makes the passage an *institution narrative*. Without it, nothing would be *instituted*: it would only be the story of Jesus' last meal before His death. But Jesus commands the Apostles to repeat the meal when He is no longer visibly present, and so the account of the Last Supper becomes the foundational story for the Church's actions, as we see in the Acts of the Apostles (2:42, 46; 20:7, 11; 27:35).

Some people say that Jesus was using the bread and wine as metaphors to explain His upcoming sacrifice. But, if that were the case, they would be useless. They fail as metaphors, because it is the bread and wine and not His death that require explanation! Jesus' words are not so much an explanation or a teaching as a "speech-act," a declaration that brings about what it expresses—like "Let there be light" or any of God's covenant promises. Jesus' speech does not come after the event; it brings about the event.

And what is implicit at the Last Supper becomes explicit in the Emmaus story, where the visible presence of the Lord vanishes during the distribution of the pieces (24:31). Why did this happen? Because, in light of Luke 22:19, His presence was now identified with the bread. Thus the messianic king was "made known" to the disciples "in the breaking of bread" (24:35). Later, Luke links his own liturgical experience to Jesus' Last Supper by including himself among those who gather on the first day of the week to "break bread" (Acts 20:7).

In the Last Supper and the Emmaus story, Christians—throughout all of history—have learned that the risen Christ is truly present in the bread we break together.

Where the Eucharist is, there is the king. And where the king is, there is the kingdom.

NEW AND IMPROVED

In Luke's Gospel, Jesus refers to the Eucharistic cup as the "*new covenant in My blood*" (22:20). He is certainly evoking Moses' words at Exodus 24:6–8, "Behold the blood of the covenant," but He is combining it with Jeremiah's much later oracle of God's promise: "Behold, the days are coming, says the Lord, when I will make a new covenant with the house of Israel and the house of Judah" (Jer 31:31). The "new covenant" of Jeremiah was to be unlike the *broken* covenant of Sinai (Jer 31:32). The prophet made clear (in Jer 30–33) that the "new covenant" would involve a new level of intimacy with God (31:33–34)—plus the reunification of the divided kingdom (31:31) and *the restoration of the House of David* (30:9; 33:14–26) and the *covenant of David* (33:19–21). That's big news; it's good news; and it's all caught up in Jesus' words of institution.

With these covenantal associations, Jesus marks this meal as a *covenant-renewal* meal, just as the Passover was the covenant-renewal meal of God's covenant with Moses. When Christians take the Eucharistic cup, they reaffirm their place within the covenant—the renewed and transformed Davidic covenant.

Within this renewed kingdom, Jesus will share His authority, but not before He corrects the disciples' misguided notions of kingship and power (Lk 22:28–30). He tells them: "I assign to you, as My Father assigned to Me, a kingdom" (v. 29). The verb translated as "assign" does not quite capture the sense of the Greek. The original word, *diatithemai*, means literally "to make a covenant." A more precise translation of the sentence would be "I covenant to you a kingdom, as My Father covenanted one to Me, that you may eat and drink at My table in My kingdom, and sit on thrones judging the twelve tribes of Israel" (Lk 22:29–30).

The clarification of that verb may seem like a small change, but it really adds an astonishing element to an already remarkable list of Davidic privileges that Jesus is passing on to His Apostles: the thrones, the tribes, the father-son relationship, the banquet at the king's table—and now the covenant.

For Scripture tells us of only one kingdom that had been founded on a covenant: the kingdom of David (see Ps 89:3–4, 28–37). Only the kingdom of David enjoyed that family bond with God Himself. But now Jesus is extending the covenant as He renews it.

The meaning of Luke 22:29 becomes clear: since Jesus is the son of David, He is the legal heir to David's covenant and throne. God has "covenanted" to Him a kingdom. Now Jesus, through the "new covenant in [His] blood," is "covenanting" to the disciples that same kingdom. This is not the *promise* of a conferral (future tense), but the *declaration* of a conferral (present tense).

Yet Jesus isn't giving away His kingdom. He continues to refer to it as "My kingdom." The Apostles do not replace Him in any way. But now they may share in His kingship as well as His priesthood. The very purpose of the new covenant, Jesus says, is to admit the disciples to "eat and drink at My table in My kingdom." He is sharing the exercise of authority in His kingdom with those who share in His body, His covenant, and His life. And the distinguishing mark of that authority is service. Jesus Himself is not seated, but rather serving the others.

The sign of the kingdom will be eating and drinking at the king's table. But note that the disciples are already—at the Last Supper—eating and drinking at Jesus' table. He is not putting it off till a future date. The sign of the kingdom is there, present tense, in the Upper Room.

What can this mean? It means that *the kingdom is already present in the Eucharistic eating and drinking*. And the presence of the kingdom continues when the Apostles break bread in remembrance of Jesus. The celebration of the Eucharist manifests the kingdom. Kingdom and Eucharist are tightly bound: God's kingdom is a *Eucharistic kingdom*.

Jesus is the heir of the covenant with David. He is eternal king over Israel and the nations (Lk 1:32–33). But now He enacts a *new* covenant between Himself and the disciples, extending the privileges of God's covenant beyond the House of David, to all the Apostles. The Apostles, like Christ, are now heirs of the kingdom of David. And, because they are heirs, they enjoy the privileges of God's children: they eat at the royal table and sit on the thrones of the royal house, judging the twelve tribes.

It's all about the kingdom of David. It's all about the kingdom of God. It's all about the Church. And it's all about you and me.

For Christ made it clear: the kingdom of God is the Church, and it belongs to God's children. For "the children share in the flesh and blood" (Heb 2:14) of the great king.

ACTING UP

What does this mean for the Church? We find out immediately and repeatedly in the Acts of the Apostles.

Jesus' promise of inheritance and rulership is fulfilled as the Apostles assume authority in the Church. What's more, the promise of table fellowship is fulfilled, first, in post-resurrection meals with Jesus and then in the Church's continuing Eucharistic practice.

In the very first verses of Acts (1:3, 6), we learn that Jesus' topic of discussion with the Apostles over forty days was *the kingdom of God*. "Kingdom" will remain a central theme throughout the book, which ends with Paul proclaiming the kingdom of God in Rome (28:31). Acts 1:4 makes the now-familiar connection between the kingdom and eating and drinking—the messianic banquet—when it states that Jesus taught them over this forty-day period "while taking salt" with them. "Taking salt" is slang for "eating together."

When the disciples ask Jesus, "Lord, will You at this time restore the kingdom to Israel?" (1:6), they may be referring to Jesus' promise in Luke 22:30 that "you will sit on thrones." If that is so, then the Apostles are asking, "When will we receive the authority promised to us?" While Jesus discourages speculation about *timing* (v. 7), He does in fact describe the *means* by which the kingdom will be restored, namely, through the Spirit-inspired witness of the Apostles throughout the earth (v. 8). Jesus' geographical description of their mission—"in Jerusalem and in all Judea and Samaria and to the end of the earth"—is, on the one hand, a programmatic outline of the narrative of Acts, helping us recognize that the whole book concerns the spread of the kingdom (cf. Acts 28:31). But, on the other hand, it is a *Davidic map* that reflects the *theological geography* of God's covenant pledge concerning the extent of the Davidic empire. Jerusalem was David's city (2 Sam 5:6–10), Judea his tribal land (2 Sam 5:5; 1 Kgs 12:21); Samaria represented northern Israel, David's nation (1 Kgs 12:16); and "the ends of the earth" stood for the Gentiles (cf. Is. 49:6), David's vassals (Ps 2:7–8; 72:8–12; 89:25–27).

Still, the Apostles did not yet understand what Jesus was saying. They did not know that He would transform their *expectation* of a national, earthly kingdom to the *realization* of a kingdom that is international, universal, catholic—a kingdom that is manifest on earth, but essentially heavenly. *The Spirit must still be poured out before the Apostles can perceive the transformed kingdom.* Thus, only *after* the disciples have received the power of the Holy Spirit will they become true witnesses (Acts 1:8).

Between the promise of the Spirit (Acts 1:8) and Pentecost (2:1–4), Luke records the restoration of the circle of the Twelve by the replacement of Judas with Matthias. Once the Twelve have been reconstituted, the event of Pentecost (Acts 2:1–42) marks the restoration of Israel as kingdom under the Son of David, and the beginning of the Apostles' vice-regency over that kingdom.

Luke vividly shows us the promised restoration of the kingdom. Not only are all the Twelve (and presumably the hundred and twenty) "all together in one place" (2:1)—thus representing the nucleus of the restored Israel—but they address their message to "Jews, devout men from every nation under heaven" (v. 5); and Luke enumerates those nations (vv. 9–11). In a moment, the work of the Apostles reverses the effects of the exile and dispersion of the tribes.

Thus the prophecies of Joel (Jl 2:28–32) and others are fulfilled, and Israel is restored, not definitively—as the Church still must grow much more—but nonetheless fundamentally. God has gathered the scattered children of Israel. And, for the chosen people, that in-gathering was the very definition of salvation.

In Acts we see that the restored Israel had a certain form and structure: not that of the confederated tribes at Sinai, but that of the twelve tribes within the *kingdom of David*. Peter's sermon stresses the Davidic royalty of Jesus Christ (Acts 2:36). He preaches to the assembled exiles of Israel that Jesus is the fulfillment of the covenant of David (v. 30) and the fulfillment of David's own prophecies (vv. 25–28, 34–35). He applies to Jesus the royal enthronement psalm (Psalm 110), asserting that Jesus is now enthroned in heaven ("exalted at the right hand of God") and has poured out the Spirit on the Apostles as the crowd has just witnessed (v. 33). Thus, Jesus is reigning *now* in heaven, and the results of His reign are being manifest *now* in events that the people may "see and hear" (v. 33).

Peter and the Apostles, filled with the Spirit, have become witnesses. Now they see the nature of Jesus' kingdom and its present realization. When Peter's hearers accept the fact that Jesus is the Davidic king—and thus acknowledge His rightful reign over themselves—they are incorporated into the Church through baptism (2:41–42; see also 4:32–5:11, esp. 5:11).

It is important to note, however, that the Davidic kingdom is not only restored, but also transformed. The Son of David is not enthroned in the earthly Jerusalem, but the heavenly, "exalted at the right hand of God." The kingdom has been transposed from earth to heaven, even though it continues to manifest itself on earth as the Church. The kingdom—the Church—exists simultaneously on earth and in heaven. The king is enthroned in heaven, but His ministers (the Apostles) are active on earth. Meanwhile, the heavenly king is united to His earthly officers and subjects by the Holy Spirit and by the sacraments, especially baptism and the Eucharist (Acts 2:38–42).

The Davidic kingdom finds historic fulfillment in the Catholic Church. Yet it also undergoes a transposition from the earthly to the heavenly sphere. The earthly Jerusalem and its Temple, despite Luke's genuine respect for them, cannot be the kingdom's ultimate fulfillment (see Acts 7:48–50; Lk. 21:6). Peter makes clear that Christ's present rule is not from the earthly Jerusalem, but from the heavenly (Acts 2:33). Nonetheless, His reign expresses itself in the earthly realm by what can be "seen and heard" (Acts 2:33). The renewed kingdom of David, of which the Church is the visible manifestation, exists simultaneously in heaven and on earth, as its citizens move from one sphere to the other.

Still, the whole kingdom—the whole Church—is united by the indwelling Holy Spirit and the celebration of the Eucharist. That's when the king becomes present, when the kingdom is manifest, and when the earthly citizens of the kingdom participate in the perpetual messianic banquet of the heavenly king.

NET WORTH, FIELD OF DREAMS

It's all new. Yet it was all there, as if in seed, in the time of David. The twentieth-century Scripture scholar Father Raymond Brown points out that the united kingdom of Israel under David remains the one Israelite institution with the greatest relevance for the study of the Church today:

> The story of David brings out all the strengths and weaknesses of the beginnings of the religious institution of the kingdom for the people of God . . . *The kingdom established by David . . . is the closest Old Testament parallel to the New Testament Church* . . . To help Christians make up their mind on how the Bible speaks [to Church issues], it would help if they knew about David and his kingdom, *which was also God's kingdom* and whose kings, with all their imperfections, God promised to treat as "sons" (2 Sam 6:14).

And there are indeed imperfections in what we see of the Church. All of the kingdom's earthly rulers are imperfect, as I am, and as I suppose you are, and as David was, and as Peter was. As I said earlier in the book, the pope goes to confession at least once a week.

But *this* Church, with all its imperfections, is the only Church that can correspond both to the kingdom covenanted by Jesus and to the "kingdom parables" Jesus tells in Matthew's Gospel. With those seven parables, Jesus prepared His disciples to recognize the kingdom of heaven, and to recognize that the kingdom on earth would be a mixture of good and bad—much like the original Davidic kingdom. It would be a field sown with both wheat and weeds, a dragnet brimming with good fish and rubbish.

At the same time, the parables make clear that the restored kingdom will be manifest in an unexpected form that may not be recognized by many (see Mt 13:11–15, 44–46). It will not be characterized by royal pomp, military conquest, political power, and economic wealth. Amid Pilate's interrogation, Jesus put the matter in no uncertain terms: "My kingship is not of this world; if My kingship were of this world, My servants would fight, that I might not be handed over to the Jews; but My kingship is not from the world" (Jn 18:36). Jesus did not mean His kingdom is not *in* this world, just that His kingdom does not derive its royal authority *from* this world's swords or armies or majority votes or political parties. He derives His royal authority from His heavenly Father. The kingdom was not what Caiaphas or Pilate—or any of their contemporaries—had expected.

From the kingdom parables we can conclude—beyond any doubt—that Jesus established a kingdom on earth with His coming. In the fourth century, St. Augustine put it well: "The Church is already now the kingdom of Christ and the kingdom of heaven." A modern theologian, Cardinal Charles Journet, echoed him: "The kingdom is already on earth, and the Church is already in heaven. To abandon the equal value of Church and kingdom would mean overlooking this important revelation."

Thus, unless we include both the earthly and the heavenly, we are not seeing the Church (or the kingdom) as Jesus wants us to see it. For there aren't two Churches, one in heaven and one on earth. Nor are there two kingdoms, one on earth and one (for the moment) present only in heaven. The Church exists in two states, but it is one Church. It is one kingdom. There is, as we profess in the creed, only one holy, catholic, and apostolic Church.

The kingdom has come, and it is the Church—the universal Church—the Catholic Church—a field with wheat and weeds, a net with good fish and bad. If Jesus had intended the kingdom to be established in its perfection, He would not have included the weeds in that field or the bad fish in that dragnet. His parables make sense only if *the kingdom is the Church as we know it*—one, holy, catholic, and apostolic—full of sinners, some of us repentant.

Only in heaven, at the end of time, will we know the kingdom in its manifest glory: "when He appears we shall be like Him, for we shall see Him as He is" (I Jn 3:2). Until that day, He is still with us in all His glory, in the Church, the Eucharistic kingdom. For it's not that He's less glorious now. It's just that we cannot perceive Him as He is.

Still, "we are God's children now" (I Jn 3:2), thanks to the covenant. We are sons of God in the Davidic "Son of God," the king of creation. And that is ample cause for rejoicing from now until the day when the Son of David heals us, that we might see (see Lk 18:41), and so see His glory.

JERUSALEM, MY HAPPY HOME

The Old Testament foresaw our day and foreshadowed it. Even in the time of David, the Greek Septuagint Bible tells us, when the priest-king gathered to worship with the assembly of Israel, he gathered with the *ekklesia*. That's the word the New Testament uses to denote the Church. And so the priest-king gathers with the Church today. But where?

By now, we should not be surprised to learn that, when we go to Mass, we go to the habitation of King David: "you have come to *Mount Zion* and to the city of the living God, the *heavenly Jerusalem*, and to innumerable angels in festal gathering, and to the assembly [*ekklesia*, Church] of the firstborn" (Heb 12:22). Though the earthly Jerusalem and its Temple were destroyed just a generation after Jesus ascended to heaven, Christ Himself gave His people more than a consolation. He revealed to us the heavenly Jerusalem: "And in the Spirit he carried me away to a great, high mountain, and showed me the holy city Jerusalem coming down out of heaven from God, having the glory of God" (Rev 21:10–11), "the new Jerusalem which comes down from my God out of heaven" (Rev 3:12).

That is what happens when we celebrate the Eucharist: the new Jerusalem comes down from heaven—and God and His angels lift us up to divine life. When we go to Mass, we gather as the Church of the priest-king, a king forever, like David, a priest forever like Melchizedek. The king of Salem, the King of Peace, still reigns in the place where the bread and wine are offered to God in thanksgiving, in the *todah*, in *eucharistia*. The Son of David is really present among us, and so we are really present in His kingdom.

Mount Zion comes down from heaven! Jerusalem descends in grace to the place where you and I go to Mass, even if it is the humblest chapel, even if it's behind battlements in the open air of a foreign land. We are at home on Mount Zion. The kingdom of heaven touches down wherever we go to Mass. There we are served by apostolic ministers, vice-regents of Christ, ordained according to the apostolic custom.

The kingdom imagery dominates the Bible's Book of Revelation. It is there that we meet Jesus as "the firstborn of the dead and the ruler of the kings of the earth," recalling what is said of David in Psalm 89:27: "And I will make him the firstborn, the highest of the kings of the earth." This Jesus has "made us [to be] a kingdom" (Rev 1:6). The sword that proceeds from his mouth (Rev 1:16) refers to the Davidic prophecy of Isaiah 11:4: "[The shoot of Jesse] shall smite the earth with the rod of his mouth, and with the breath of his lips he shall slay the wicked." In Revelation 5:5, Christ appears as "the Lion of the tribe of Judah, the Root of David." The reign of this Davidic Christ is universal and eternal: "The kingdom of the world has become the kingdom of our Lord and of His Christ, and He shall reign for ever and ever" (Rev 11:5). In Revelation 12:1–6, the mother of the Christ ("a male child who is to rule all the nations with a rod of iron," v. 5; see Ps 2:8–9) is portrayed as royalty ("clothed with the sun, with the moon under her feet, and on her head a crown of twelve stars," v. 1), that is, as fulfilling the role of Israel's Queen Mother.

What we find, then, on the last page of Revelation recapitulates what we found in nature's pristine state, on the first pages of Genesis. We find divinized man given dominion over the cosmos, by means of a covenant with God. We are one with that Man in a Holy Communion. Far more than we are one with our ancestor Adam, we are one with Jesus, the Christ, the Son of God, the King.

And His kingdom is the Church. That fact might take us by surprise. But the Lord told us that it would, and well it should. Our God transcends us. So He fulfills our prayers and expectations in surprising ways and in hidden ways. That is the very definition of mystery.

What, then, of Alfred Loisy and his taunt about the Church being a poor stand-in for the kingdom? Loisy looked for evidence that Jesus intended to establish a Church, and he found it wanting.

But we might very well ask in reply: Where is the evidence that Jesus intended to abolish the structures and traditions of Israel? There is none! Jesus Himself declared emphatically: "Think not that I have come to abolish the law and the prophets; I have come not to abolish them but to fulfil them. For truly, I say to you, till heaven and earth pass away, not an iota, not a dot, will pass from the law until all is accomplished. Whoever then relaxes one of the least of these commandments and teaches men so, shall be called least in the kingdom of heaven; but he who does them and teaches them shall be called great in the kingdom of heaven" (Mt 5:17–19). The question we should ask is this: what would those traditions and structures look like if their penultimate, Davidic form were fulfilled in a way that is both restorative and transformative?

Fifteen

THE CATHOLIC LIFETIME READINGS PLAN

An Apologetic Exhortation

"Always be prepared to make a defense to any one who calls you to account for the hope that is in you, yet do it with gentleness and reverence" (1 Pet 3:15).

Gentleness and reverence come naturally and supernaturally to those who know they are living in the kingdom. We are always in the presence of the holy, and we see in all others the image of our immortal king.

We should always be ready with an answer. But this is what should set Catholic apologists apart: we answer to *lift people up*, not shut them up. If we genuinely listen to people who disagree with us, and if we learn to present the content of the Catholic faith to them in a positive way, we are far more likely to persuade them. Sometimes, in the midst of an argument, we can get so caught up in the mechanics of argumentation that we miss many opportunities to witness to grace.

Just as It Should Be

The great nineteenth-century theologian Matthias Scheeben said that something like that happened in the centuries after the Protestant Reformation. Both Catholics and Protestants, he said, got so caught up in their debates that they produced misshapen theologies and misleading witness; because, instead of focusing on the essentials of faith, they dwelt on the points in dispute. Scheeben noted that the Council of Trent (echoing St. Paul in Rom 8:14–17) had provided a serious and considerate answer to Protestant questions on justification—but Catholics ignored it! They were so busy formulating a response in the legal terms that the reformers were using that they missed the transcendent beauty of Trent's doctrine.

Trent defined justification as "a transference from the state in which man is born a son of the first Adam, to the state of grace and adoption of the sons of God." If Catholics had used the language of Trent, Scheeben said,

> the notion of justification would have escaped the shallow
> and muddled treatment that has so often disfigured it.
> Many inverted the proper procedure. Instead of starting
> with an adequate idea of God's adoptive sonship and then
> determining the concept of justice contained in this idea,
> they preferred to regard divine sonship as a relationship to
> God arising from human justice, which they looked upon as
> a right disposition connected with freedom from sin, and
> an inclination toward morally good conduct. Thereby they
> did away with the possibility of fixing upon anything
> supernatural in this justice, and could conceive of the

divine sonship itself only in an extremely vague, if not altogether rationalist, fashion. But if we follow the Council of Trent, and if with the Council we focus our attention on the fact that at bottom justification is a transition to the state of an adoptive child, to the state of the children of God, it emerges before our eyes with its greatness unimpaired.

This was a missed opportunity of massive proportions. Luther had described justification as "the doctrine by which the Church stands or falls" and "the chief article of the whole Christian doctrine, which comprehends the ruler and judge over all other Christian doctrines." Luther argued his case from Pauline texts, emphasizing "that a man is justified by faith apart from works of law" (Rom 3:28). So emphatic was Luther about the worthlessness of human works that he inserted the word "alone" after "faith" when he translated Paul's text, claiming that salvation is by "faith alone." Yet the phrase "faith alone" actually appears in only one place in Scripture, and that is in the Letter of James, which explicitly denies what would later become Luther's keystone of doctrine: "You see that a man is justified by works and not by faith alone" (Jas 2:24). Luther dealt with the problem by proposing to remove James from his New Testament; later theologians argued that Paul and James meant different things when they used the verb "justified."

The semantic differences between James and Paul are debatable at best. The semantic differences between Protestant and Catholic dogmatists, however, are a fact of history. And Catholics could have avoided much of it if they had simply followed Trent in placing their own accent on the idea of divine filiation—the astonishing fact that Christians are, by grace, adopted sons of God. As St.

John of Damascus put it in the eighth century: in baptism, we become by grace what God is by nature.

Trent's approach also would have enabled us to speak of justification in the "covenantal" terms favored by John Calvin and his division of the Reformation. For Luther and Calvin, as for St.
Augustine and the Council of Trent, you have to experience divine
regeneration before you can exercise the faith that justifies. Regeneration precedes justification. Generation is how we come into the
natural family as children. Regeneration, through baptism, is how
we come to God's family.

It is only in recent decades that Catholic theologians and ecu-
menists have earnestly begun to employ the methods proposed by
Trent. And the results have been remarkable. On the institutional
level, we have seen the world's Lutherans sign a "Joint Declaration
on Justification." On the personal level, a great many Lutherans—
both clergy and laity, and even some very prominent theologians—
have recently come into full communion with the Catholic Church
(notably Richard John Neuhaus, Reinhard Hütter, Bruce Marshall,
Mickey Mattox, Leonard Klein, and Jennifer Mehl Ferrara).

MASS CONVERSIONS

The lesson from history should be clear to us. So much depends
upon our *deep, personal* appropriation of the faith—in positive biblical terms—and in the Church's own terms! We must make the
biblical and Catholic doctrine our own, through study and prayer.
(The first conversion we must seek—always—is our own.) And
then we must strive to present our faith in a positive way, rather
than in a simply reactionary way.

Sometimes we may answer with a single verse, because that's
what our friends are looking for; but the true Catholic answer is

the entire Bible. Sometimes we may answer in a single breath; but we must also answer with our entire lives. For we are servants, like Christ. We are witnesses, like His holy Apostles. Only if we are saints and servants and witnesses will we be true apologists—and, more than that, true evangelists.

Evangelization is not the work of arguments alone. People need to see the reality of the kingdom when they see the Church and see her members, and even the most clearly formulated doctrine cannot force anyone to see what our own sins have obscured. The Catechism echoes St. Thomas Aquinas when it says: "We do not believe in formulas, but in those realities they express, which faith allows us to touch. The believer's act of faith does not terminate in the propositions, but in the realities which they express" (CCC, n. 170). Our apostolic goal, then, is to manifest the kingdom. Giving a more convincing reason doesn't make the truth of the kingdom more real, just more accessible.

We have many reasons to believe. We have plausible, good, and beautiful reasons to believe. And many of our friends, neighbors, and coworkers are desperate to find a reason to believe. Our words and our lives should give them ample reasons.

As Father Scheeben noted, though, all our reasons come down to one: We are God's children now. Divine filiation—our family relationship with God—is a key that unlocks so many of the mysteries and enigmas of Scripture—and opens the door to a more positive and effective apologetics. Once we see ourselves as God's children, the other mysteries fall into place. Baptism? It is our birth into the family. The Mass? It is our family meal, our holy sacrifice at the altar of our true home. The saints? They are our siblings. The Blessed Virgin? She is our mother. The pope? As God's vicar, he is our holy father. The kingdom? It is ours because it belongs to the Son of God. The Church? It is our home, because it is the kingdom of heaven, and the kingdom of heaven belongs to children like us!

People sometimes ask me what is the best way to prepare for the task of apologetics. Well, we should all be doing certain things: praying, reading the Scriptures, seeking wisdom from reliable teachers, and seeking the grace of the Holy Spirit, to name just a few. But we can also take a "shortcut," because there's one practice that encompasses all those others.

If I had to name only one preparation for the work of apologetics, it would be this: full, conscious, and active participation in the Holy Mass. Go as often as you can. Of course, we must go on Sundays and holy days. But go on weekdays, too, if you can do it in a way that doesn't threaten your employment or burden your family.

The Mass is where we grow familiar with the contours of reality. It's where the natural world—of wheat, wine, and water—meets the supernatural, and where they coexist in one kingdom, with the angels crying out "Holy, holy, holy!" before the consecrated elements. It's in the Mass that *we are set apart*, along with those elements of nature, to be consecrated, to be holy, to be divinized.

The Mass is where the Bible dwells in its natural and supernatural habitat. The Mass is where the whole Bible hangs together, and it's the only place where the whole Bible is proclaimed consistently and fully. For the Mass is the culmination of the Bible's prophecy. The Bible is about the Mass, and the Bible suffuses the Mass. When we go to Mass often, we absorb the Bible, as if through every pore of our body. We take it in with the grace to understand it.

I'll tell you about my early experience of this.

KEYS TO THE KINGDOM

I was a new Catholic, and I was flush with the pride of discovery.

I'd just presented a paper to a doctoral seminar on the Gospel of Matthew, and I thought my work was important and original. I also believed it was true. Even the grueling, two-and-a-half-hour session of questioning by my professor and fellow students had left me—and my thesis—unscathed.

What was the subject? I argued that Matthew's account of Jesus giving Peter the "keys to the kingdom" cites the obscure oracle of Isaiah about the transfer of "the key of the House of David." What Jesus conferred upon Peter—namely, authority over His Church—corresponded to what Isaiah's king had conferred upon Eliakim in making him prime minister of the Davidic kingdom. In both cases there was an office with both primacy and succession. When one person vacated the office, another took his place, and the successor held authority identical to that of his predecessor.

Earlier scholars, both Protestant and Catholic, had noticed the Isaiah citation. And you don't have to be a scholar to notice that Matthew is filled with quotations, citations, allusions, and echoes from the Old Testament.

I felt I had a fresh insight, however, in seeing how the citation helps us understand Matthew's meaning and Jesus' intention. As I saw it, the passage depicted Jesus as the new Davidic king and the Church as the restored kingdom of David.

It was this conclusion and others like it that eventually led me to become a Catholic. I thanked God for the grace. But I also congratulated myself for conducting such an impressive work of scholarship. My classmates and professor may have been impressed, but not half as impressed as I was.

Yet it was only a short time later that I encountered those same two biblical passages again—in a setting I was hardly expecting.

It happened at Mass on the twenty-first Sunday in Ordinary Time. The first reading was taken from Isaiah 22, the same obscure oracle I'd studied in such detail for my paper. It is such an odd passage that I didn't expect to hear it included in the liturgy. But then, a few minutes later, the priest proclaimed the Gospel—and it was Matthew 16, the story of Jesus giving the keys to Peter!

What were the odds of those two Scriptures being read at the same Mass? I asked myself. I felt as if I'd won some kind of lectionary lottery.

Only later did I discover that the readings we hear at Mass aren't chosen by holy happenstance. My innovative interpretation of Matthew 16 was one that Catholics had been hearing in the liturgy for years—and not only scholars, but laborers, merchants, and the poorest of the poor.

It's more than twenty years now since I became a Catholic, and I've had this experience again and again at Mass.

Sunday after Sunday, the Church gives us a pattern of biblical interpretation, showing us how the promises of the Old Testament are fulfilled in the New Testament. And the Church presents the Scriptures this way because the New Testament writers did. And the New Testament writers learned it from Jesus.

The Evangelists understood the Old Testament as *salvation history*, the patient unfolding of God's gracious and merciful plan to fashion the human race into a covenant family—the family of God that worships and dwells in His kingdom.

Surely it was that promise of divine sonship that captivated me and held me, all those years ago, when I first went searching after reasons to believe, when I first sought the deeper meaning of the Church's baptism.

"Truly, truly, I say to you, unless one is born anew, he cannot *see* the kingdom of God . . . Truly, truly, I say to you, unless one is born of water and the Spirit, he cannot *enter* the kingdom of God" (Jn 3:3,5).

I learned from my first teachers that baptism is a *christening*. It is an anointing. It confers a kingship that Christ has seen fit to share with a beggar like me. More than that, it is a kingship that He wants us all to share with everyone we meet, especially those who are most hostile. Always with gentleness and reverence. And full of hope.

Notes

CHAPTER I

9. **But that's another story:** See Scott and Kimberly Hahn, *Rome Sweet Home* (San Francisco: Ignatius Press, 1993).

10. **Specifically, we're talking about that branch of theology known as apologetics:** For an excellent overview of the importance and role of apologetics in Church history, Avery Cardinal Dulles, *History of Apologetics* (San Francisco: Ignatius Press, 2005).

10. **Students of history perhaps know:** A book containing interesting studies of the early apologists is Mark Edwards et al. (eds.), *Apologetics in the Roman Empire* (New York: Oxford University Press, 1999). For relevant selections from the early Church Fathers see Henry Chadwick, *Early Christian Thought in the Roman Empire* (New York: Oxford University Press, 1966).

11. **"whatever is true is ours":** Justin's words, in his *Second Apology* (chapter 13), are most precisely translated as "Whatever things were rightly said among all men, are the property of us Christians."

11. **Justin could treat almost everything he encountered as "seeds of the Word":** *Second Apology*, chapter 8.

11. **Well, like those ancient fathers, we live in a culture that is baffled by Christianity:** See Robert L. Wilken, *The Christians as the Romans Saw Them* (New Haven: Yale University Press, 2003).

11. **The historian Lionel Trilling, an agnostic:** Lionel Trilling, "Wordsworth and the Rabbis," in *The Opposing Self* (New York: Harcourt, 1978).

12. **We're not looking for the quick comeback:** For helpful treatments on some of the more "personal" aspects of apologetics, see Patrick Madrid, *Search and Rescue: How to Bring Your Family and Friends Into, or Back Into, the Catholic Church* (Manchester: Sophia Institute Press, 2001); and Mark Brumley, *How Not to Share Your Faith: The Seven Deadly Sins of Apologetics* (El Cajon, CA: Catholic Answers, 2002).

12. **If our defense does not flow from deep preparation:** See Frank Sheed and Maisie Ward, *Catholic Evidence Training Outlines: A Classic Guide to Understanding & Explaining the Truths of the Catholic Church* (Catholic Evidence Guild, 1992).

13. **"Where theology is read by the laity":** M. Eugene Boylan, *This Tremendous Lover* (Westminster, MD: Christian Classics, 1989), p. 119.

14. **I stand in awe of their achievements:** See James Akin, *The Salvation Controversy* (San Diego: Catholic Answers, 2001); Dave Armstrong, *A Biblical Defense of Catholicism* (Manchester, NH: Sophia Press, 2003); Jeff Cavins, *My Life on the Rock* (West Chester, PA: Ascension Press, 2002); David Currie, *Born Fundamentalist, Born Again Catholic* (San Francisco: Ignatius Press, 1996); George Duggan, *Beyond Reasonable Doubt* (Boston: St. Paul, 1987); Joseph C. Fenton, *We Stand with Christ: An Essay in Catholic Apologetics* (Milwaukee: Bruce Publishing, 1942); Marcus Grodi (ed.), *Journeys Home* (Zanesville, OH: Coming Home Resources; 2006); John Hardon, S.J.,

Christianity in Conflict: A Catholic View of Protestantism (Westminster, MD: Newman Press, 1959); Thomas Howard, *On Being Catholic* (San Francisco: Ignatius Press, 1997); Karl Keating, *Catholicism and Fundamentalism* (San Francisco: Ignatius Press, 1988); Peter Kreeft and Ronald K. Tacelli, *Handbook of Christian Apologetics* (Downers Grove, IL: InterVarsity Press, 1994); Patrick Madrid, *A Pocket Guide to Apologetics* (Huntington, IN: OSV Press, 2006); Rosalind Moss (ed.), *Home at Last* (San Diego: Catholic Answers, 2001); William Most, *Catholic Apologetics Today* (Rockford, IL: TAN Books, 1986), Stephen Ray, *Crossing the Tiber* (San Francisco: Ignatius Press, 1997); Alan Schreck, *Catholic and Christian* (Ann Arbor, MI: Servant Books, 2004); David Scott, *The Catholic Passion* (Chicago: Loyola Press, 2005); Mark Shea, *By What Authority* (Huntington, IN: OSV, 1996); Tim Staples, *Nuts and Bolts* (San Diego: Basilica Press, 1999).

For examples of various non-Catholic apologists and apologetical methods, see Bernard Ramm, *Varieties of Christian Apologetics* (Grand Rapids: Baker Academic, 1962); William Lane Craige, *Reasonable Faith: Christian Truth and Apologetics* (Wheaton, IL: Crossway Books, 1994); Steven B. Cowan (ed.), *Five Views on Apologetics* (Grand Rapids: Zondervan, 2000); C. S. Lewis, *The Case for Christianity* (Old Tappan, NJ: Touchstone Books, 1996); J. P. Moreland, *Scaling the Secular City: A Defense of Christianity* (Grand Rapids: Baker Academic, 1987); R. C. Sproul, John Gerstner, and Arthur Lindsley, *Classical Apologetics: A Rational Defense of the Christian Faith and a Critique of Presuppositional Apologetics* (Grand Rapids: Zondervan, 1984); Greg L. Bahnsen, *Always Ready: Directions for Defending the Faith* (Texarkana, AR: Covenant Media Foundation, 1996); Lee Strobel, *The Case for Christ: A Journalist's Personal Investigation of the Evidence for Jesus* (Grand Rapids: Zondervan, 1998); Josh McDowell, *The New Evidence that Demands a Verdict Fully Updated to Answer the Questions Challenging Christians Today* (Grand Rapids: Nelson

Reference, 1999); Norman L. Geisler, *Christian Apologetics* (Grand Rapids: Baker Academic, 1988).

CHAPTER 2

17. **"Faith and reason are like two wings"**: Pope John Paul II, Encyclical Letter *Fides et Ratio*, September 14, 1998, opening blessing; also see David R. Foster and Joseph Koterski, S.J. (eds.), *Two Wings of Catholic Thought: Essays on* Fides et Ratio (Washington, DC: CUA Press, 2003).

18. **"We must now recognize belief once more as the source of all knowledge"**: Michael Polanyi, *Personal Knowledge: Towards a Post-Critical Philosophy* (Chicago: University of Chicago Press, 1962), pp. 265–66. Also see C. T. Yu, "Covenantal Rationality and the Healing of Reason," in Paul J. Griffiths and Reinhard Hutter (eds.), *Reason and the Reasons of Faith* (New York: T & T Clark, 2005), pp. 223–40.

20. **There are excellent books that will teach you the science of logic:** For very readable yet informative introductions to the basic rules of logic, see Peter Kreeft, *Socratic Logic* (South Bend, IN: St. Augustine's Press, 2005) and D. Q. McInerny, *Logic: A Guide to Good Thinking* (New York: Random House, 2004). Also helpful is Norman Geisler and Ronald M. Brooks, *Come Let Us Reason: An Introduction to Logical Thinking* (Grand Rapids: Baker Academic, 1990).

20. **As such, they are the best starting points for dialogue:** Mortimer Adler was an extremely gifted philosopher and teacher who wrote about complex issues with unusual clarity. His book *Aristotle for Everyone: Difficult Thought Made Easy* (New York: Simon & Schuster, 1978) is very good for those wishing to see these four points examined in more detail.

21. **This difference between what the two senses "report"**: Strictly speaking, our eyes are not deceived since they accurately report the bending of light that makes the pencil itself seem bent. The error

occurs in our judgment that it is bent, a judgment that our sense of touch allows our reason to correct.

24. **"No one has ever seen a quark"**: John Polkinghorne, *Quarks, Chaos, and Christianity: Questions to Science and Religion* (New York: Crossroad, 1997), p. 98.

24. **"when good physicists often turn into bad philosophers"**: Robert H. March, *Physics for Poets* (Chicago: Contemporary Books, 1970).

25. **"who does not like to believe what he can know"**: Etienne Gilson, *Reason and Revelation in the Middle Ages* (New York: Scribner, 1938), pp. 83–84.

26. **God made our eyes, and He made them that we might see:** For an excellent treatment of the theological virtue of faith, see Romanus Cessario, O.P., *Christian Faith and the Theological Life* (Washington, DC: CUA Press, 1996); Josef Pieper, *Faith, Hope, Love* (San Francisco: Ignatius Press, 1997); Thomas Dubay, S.M., *Faith and Certitude: Can We Be Sure of the Things that Matter Most to Us?* (San Francisco: Ignatius Press, 1985). For a good examination of faith and in the broader context of Catholic history and theology, see Avery Cardinal Dulles, *The Assurance of Things Hoped For: A Theology of Christian Faith* (New York: Oxford University Press, 1994); L. Ward, *The Catholic Church and the Appeal to Reason* (New York: Macmillan, 1927).

CHAPTER 3

27. **"to engage in a similar strategy with regard to the unseen reality of God"**: Polkinghorne, *Quarks*, p. 99.

27. **"science and religion are intellectual cousins"**: Ibid., pp. 11–12.

29. **"Holy mother Church holds and teaches that God"**: First Vatican Council, Dogmatic Constitution on the Catholic Faith: *Dei Filius* 2.1 and canon 2. This affirmation turned up again in Pope Pius X's oath against modernism. More recently, the first passage from *Dei Filius* appeared verbatim in the *Catechism of the Catholic Church*, n. 36.

29. "St. Thomas Aquinas faced this problem squarely: See Gregory P. Rocca, *Speaking the Incomprehensible God: Thomas Aquinas on the Interplay of Positive and Negative Theology* (Washington, DC: CUA Press, 2004); Denys Turner, *Faith, Reason and the Existence of God* (New York: Cambridge University Press, 2004).

29. Also, whatever truth they did attain would always be mixed up with error: *Summa Contra Gentiles* I.4.1–6.

30. One particular type of fideism is called presuppositionalism: See Cornelius Van Til, *Defense of the Faith* (Phillipsburg, NJ: Presbyterian & Reformed Publishing, 1967); Thom Notaro, *Van Til's Use of Evidence* (Phillipsburg, NJ: Presbyterian & Reformed Publishing, 1980); cf. Gordon Clark, *Religion, Reason and Revelation* (Nutley, NJ: Craig Press, 1978). Another variation of the presuppositionalist approach is taken by the "reformed epistemology" school: Nicholas Wolterstorff, *Reason within the Bounds of Religion* (Grand Rapids: Eerdmans, 1984); Alvin Plantinga, *Warranted Christian Belief* (New York: Oxford University Press, 2000); Mark S. McLeod, *Rationality and Theistic Belief* (Ithaca, NY: Cornell University Press, 1993).

31. Those of St. Thomas Aquinas are perhaps the most famous: See Reginald Garrigou-Lagrange, *The One God: A Commentary on the First Part of St. Thomas' Theological Summa* (St. Louis: B. Herder Book Co., 1943); *God: His Existence and His Nature*, 2 vols. (St. Louis: B. Herder Book Co., 1946).

32. St. Thomas begins his Five Ways with the "argument from motion": St. Thomas Aquinas, *Summa Theologiae*, I, q. 2, a.3). For an excellent treatment of Aquinas's understanding of the *preambula fidei*, see Ralph McInerny, *Preambula Fidei: Thomism and the God of the Philosophers* (Washington, DC: CUA Press, 2006).

34. The fifth way is the "argument from design": For a precise treatment of the proper sense of "finality" (or "design"), see Benedict M. Ashley, *The Way Toward Wisdom: An Interdisciplinary and Intercultural*

Introduction to Metaphysics (Notre Dame, IN: University of Notre Dame Press, 2006), pp. 322–81. For an explanation of "intelligent design" and the "irreducible complexity" of the created order, see Michael Behe, *Darwin's Black Box* (New York: Free Press, 2006).

34. **Even in Darwinism, nature observes a process of selection:** See Etienne Gilson, *From Aristotle to Darwin and Back Again: A Journey in Final Causality, Species, and Evolution* (Notre Dame, IN: Notre Dame University Press, 1984).

36. **"Let us weigh up the gain and the loss involved in calling heads that God exists":** Blaise Pascal, *Pensées*, tr. A. J. Krailshemer (New York: Penguin, 1966), p. 151.

37. **Yet, as C. S. Lewis noted, human beings long for something that nothing in the world can satisfy:** C. S. Lewis, *Mere Christianity* (London: Fontana, 1962), p. 118.

37. **They conclude with the caveat: "You either see this one or you don't":** *Handbook of Christian Apologetics*, p. 81.

38. **Any of these paths can take our friends above and beyond the everyday:** See Montague Brown, *Restoration of Reason: The Eclipse and Recovery of Truth, Goodness, and Beauty* (Grand Rapids: Baker Academic Press, 2006); John Saward, *The Beauty of Holiness and the Holiness of Beauty* (San Francisco: Ignatius Press, 1997).

38. **The great Dominican theologian Romanus Cessario:** Romanus Cessario, *Christian Faith and the Theological Life* (Washington, DC: Catholic University of America Press, 1996), pp. 78–79. Also see Rene Latrourelle, "Miracle," and Rino Fisichella, "Prophecy," in Rene Latourelle and Rino Fisichella (eds.), *Dictionary of Fundamental Theology* (New York: Crossroad, 1994), pp. 690–709, 788–98.

CHAPTER 4

41. **They say, for example, that "there are no absolutes":** For engaging treatments of the issues surrounding moral relativism, see Francis J.

Beckwith and Gregory Koukl, *Relativism: Feet Firmly Planted in Mid-Air* (Grand Rapids: Baker Books, 1998); Peter Kreeft, *A Refutation of Moral Relativism: Interviews with an Absolutist* (San Francisco: Ignatius Press, 1999).

43. **These norms witness to something that philosophers:** See Russell Hittinger, *The First Grace: Rediscovering the Natural Law in the Post-Christian World* (Wilmington, DE: ISI Books, 2003); J. Budziszewski, *Written on the Heart: The Case for Natural Law* (Downers Grove: InterVarsity Press, 1997); Charles E. Rice, *50 Questions on the Natural Law: What It Is, and Why We Need It* (San Francisco: Ignatius Press, 1999); Oscar J. Brown, *Natural Rectitude and Divine Law in Aquinas: An Approach to an Integral Interpretation of the Thomistic Doctrine of Law* (Toronto: Pontifical Institute of Mediaeval Studies, 1981); Heinrich A. Rommen, *The Natural Law: A Study in Legal and Social History and Philosophy* (Indianapolis: Liberty Fund, 1998); Fulvio Di Blasi, *God and the Natural Law: A Rereading of Thomas Aquinas* (South Bend, IN: St. Augustine's Press, 2006).

45. **Nevertheless, if atheism is not *at root* an intellectual problem:** See Paul Vitz, *Faith of the Fatherless: The Psychology of Atheism* (Dallas: Spence Publishing, 1999); R. C. Sproul, *The Psychology of Atheism* (Minneapolis: Bethany Fellowship, 1974); John P. Koster, *The Atheist Syndrome* (Brentwood, TN: Wolgemuth & Hyatt, 1989); Ravi Zacharias, *The Real Face of Atheism* (Grand Rapids: Baker Books, 2004); Alister McGrath, *The Twilight of Atheism: The Rise and Fall of Disbelief in the Modern World* (New York: Doubleday, 2004).

50. **It is a diminishment, a privation:** See St. Thomas Aquinas, *On Evil*, q. I, a.I.

51. **To move beyond this problem, we need to move from the philosophical to the theological:** For a philosophical propaedeutic for what follows, see Daniel McInerny, *The Difficult Good: A Thomistic*

Approach to Moral Conflict and Human Happiness (New York: Fordham University Press, 2006).

52. **The grace He gave us was His own sonship:** For a valuable study of how God achieves a greater good by allowing sin, see Thomas Hibbs, *Dialectic and Narrative in Aquinas* (Notre Dame, IN: University of Notre Dame Press, 1995), pp. 134–77. On divine grace as our sharing in Christ's divine sonship, see especially Matthias Scheeben, *The Mysteries of Christianity* (St. Louis: Herder, 1946); also Dom Wulstan Mork, *Transformed by Grace: Scripture, Sacraments, and the Sonship of Christ*; Columba Marmion, *Christ, The Life of the Soul* (Bethesda: Zaccheus Press, 2005); William K. McDonough, *The Divine Family: The Trinity and Our Life in God* (Cincinnati: Servant Books, 2005); F. Fernandez-Carvajal and Peter Beteta, *Children of God* (Princeton, NJ: Scepter Publishers, 1997).

52. **That's why God let us fall:** See Richard A. White, "Sola Gratia, Solo Christo: The Roman Catholic Doctrine of Justification" (http://www.salvationhistory.com/library/apologetics/SolaGratia SoloChristo.cfm); Richard A. White, "Justification as Divine Sonship: Is 'Faith Alone' Justifiable?" in *Catholic for a Reason: Scripture and the Mystery of the Family of God*, ed. Scott Hahn and Leon J. Suprenant Jr. (Steubenville, OH: Emmaus Road Publishing, 1998), pp. 93–111; Christopher J. Malloy, *Engrafted into Christ: A Critique of the Joint Declaration* (New York: Peter Lang Publishing, 2005); Paul O'Callaghan, *Fides Christi: The Justification Debate* (Dublin, Ireland: Four Courts Press, 1997).

53. **The virtues are nothing but forms of love:** See Servais Pinckaers, *The Sources of Christian Ethics* (Washington, DC: Catholic University of America Press, 1995); Romanus Cessario, *The Virtues, Or the Examined Life* (New York: Continuum, 2002).

54. **For "we are children of God":** See Norbert Hoffmann,

"Atonement and the Ontological Coherence between the Trinity
and the Cross," in *Towards a Civilization of Love: A Symposium on the
Scriptural and Theological Foundations of the Devotion to the Heart of Jesus*, ed.
Mario Luigi Ciappi (San Francisco: Ignatius Press, 1985), pp.
213–66; Norbert Hoffmann, "Atonement and the Spirituality of
the Sacred Heart: An Attempt at an Elucidation by Means of the
Principle of 'Representation,' " in *Faith in Christ and the Worship of
Christ*, ed. Leo Scheffczyk (San Francisco: Ignatius Press, 1986), pp.
141–206.

CHAPTER 5

60. **One of early Christianity's most persuasive arguments:** See Oskar
Skarsaune, *Proof from Prophecy: A Study in Justin Martyr's Proof-Text
Tradition* (Leiden: Brill 1987).

62. **The proof from prophecy offers powerful reasons to believe:** On
this key notion, see J. C. Fenton, *We Stand with Christ*, pp. 64–99;
H. D. Gardeil, *La Credibilite et l'Apolgetique* (Paris: Cerf, 1928).

CHAPTER 6

68. **"Don't bother me . . . I'm looking for a verse of Scripture":** Both
cartoons appear in Schulz's book *What Was Bugging Ol' Pharaoh?*
(Anderson, IN: Warner, 1964), unnumbered pages.

69. **Catholics, on the other hand, hold that the New Testament
established certain institutions:** See Mark Shea, *By What Authority?
An Evangelical Discovers Catholic Tradition* (Huntington, IN: Our Sunday
Visitor, 1996); Robert Sungenis, ed., *Not By Scripture Alone: A Catholic
Critique of the Protestant Doctrine of* Sola Scriptura (Santa Barbara, CA:
Queenship Publishing Company, 1998); Yves M.-J. Congar, *Tradition
and Traditions: The Biblical, Historical, and Theological Evidence for Catholic
Teaching on Tradition* (San Diego: Basilica Press, 1997); Yves M.-J.
Congar, *The Meaning of Tradition* (San Francisco: Ignatius Press,

2004); Louis Bouyer, *The Word, Church, and Sacraments: In Protestantism and Catholicism* (San Francisco: Ignatius Press, 2004).

71. **We can proceed in at least qualified agreement on several key points:** On ritual worship and human nature, see two very different but complementary studies: R. A. Rappaport, *Ritual and Religion in the Making of Humanity* (New York: Cambridge University Press, 1999); Z. J. Zdybicka, *Person and Religion* (New York: Peter Lang, 1991).

74. **We should not, moreover, be afraid to affirm a high view of the historical value of the Bible:** See Scott Hahn, *Letter and Spirit: From Written Text to Living Word in the Liturgy* (New York: Doubleday, 2005), pp. 78–83, 187–89. See also Dean P. Béchard, ed., *The Scripture Documents: An Anthology of Official Catholic Teachings* (Collegeville, MN: Liturgical Press, 2002); Augustin Cardinal Bea, *The Word of God and Mankind* (Chicago: Franciscan Herald Press, 1967); Brian W. Harrison, O.S., *The Teaching of Pope Paul VI on Sacred Scripture with Special Reference to the Historicity of the Gospels* (Rome: Pontificium Athenaeum Sanctae Crucis, 1997); Cardinal Paul Y. Taguchi, *The Study of Sacred Scripture* (Boston: Daughters of St. Paul, 1974); William G. Most, *Free from All Error: Authorship, Inerrancy, Historicity of Scripture, Church Teaching, and Modern Scripture Scholars* (Libertyville, IL: Franciscan Marytown Press, 1985).

75. **Kenneth Kitchen's book *On the Reliability of the Old Testament* should satisfy critics:** Kenneth Kitchen, *On the Reliability of the Old Testament* (Grand Rapids: Wm. B. Eerdmans Publishing Co., 2003); also see Walter Kaiser, *The Old Testament Documents: Are They Reliable and Relevant?* (Downers Grove, IL: InterVarsity Press, 2001).

75. **The agnostic historian William Dever:** See his *What Did the Biblical Writers Know and When Did They Know It?: What Archaeology Can Tell Us about the Reality of Ancient Israel* (Grand Rapids: Wm. B. Eerdmans Publishing Co., 2001); *Who Were the Early Israelites and Where Did They Come From?* (Grand Rapids: Wm. B. Eerdmans Publishing Co.,

2006); *Recent Archaeological Discoveries and Biblical Research* (Seattle: University of Washington Press, 1989).

75. **N. T. Wright is a profound and prolific expositor:** See his *The New Testament and the People of God* (Minneapolis: Fortress Press, 1992); *Jesus and the Victory of God* (Minneapolis: Fortress Press, 1996); *The Resurrection of the Son of God* (Minneapolis: Fortress Press, 2003); *What Saint Paul Really Said: Was Paul of Tarsus the Real Founder of Christianity?* (Grand Rapids: Wm. B. Eerdmans Publishing Co., 1997); *Simply Christian: Why Christianity Makes Sense* (San Francisco: HarperCollins, 2006).

77. **The Church that canonized the Scriptures was the very Church:** See Scott Hahn, "Canon, Cult, and Covenant," in Craig Bartholomew and S. W. Hahn (eds.), *Canon and Biblical Interpretation,* (Grand Rapids: Zondervan, 2006), pp. 207–35. See also Hahn, *Letter and Spirit,* pp. 46–52.

84. **He pointed out that temporary abstinence was a condition:** For Aphrahat's discussion of celibacy, see the translation of Demonstration XVIII, on virginity and sanctity, included in Jacob Neusner, *Aphrahat and Judaism* (Leiden: Brill, 1971), pp. 78–83.

84. **This sign of holiness is prominent in the Scriptures:** See Lucien Legrand, *The Biblical Doctrine of Virginity* (New York: Sheed & Ward, 1963).

85. **Ignatius of Antioch wrote to the Christians of Smyrna:** *Letter to the Smyrnaeans* 8.2.

85. **A few years later, the word appears:** *Martyrdom of Polycarp,* salutation.

86. **Around the year 150, St. Justin noted:** *Dialogue with Trypho* 41.

86. **That line appears in the earliest Eucharistic prayers we know:** *Didache* 14. On the dating of the *Didache,* see Enrico Mazza, *The Origins of the Eucharistic Prayer* (Collegeville, MN: Liturgical Press, 1995), pp. 40–41.

86. **But the universal Church looks to Rome:** While still a Protestant,

Dr. William Farmer demonstrated that the blood of Peter and Paul is what consecrated the city of Rome as holy ground. See his book *Peter and Paul and the Church of Rome: The Ecumenical Potential of a Forgotten Perspective* (Mahwah, NJ: Paulist, 1990).

87. **"You will give us joy and gladness if you render obedience":** *To the Corinthians* 63.2.

87. **Around 105, St. Ignatius of Antioch addressed the Roman Church:** *To the Romans* 1.

87. **A few years later, in 190 A.D., St. Irenaeus:** *Against the Heresies* 3.3.2.

87. **In the following centuries, we see that the great names of Christianity:** See St. Basil, Letter 70, to Pope Damasus; for an account of Athanasius's appeal to Pope Julius I, see Socrates, *Ecclesiastical History* 2.15; for Chrysostom's appeal to Pope Innocent I, see Palladius, *Dialogue* 2; for Cyril's appeal to Pope Celestine I, see Cyril's Letter 11; St. Augustine's appeals to Rome were many, see, for example, his Letter 241, addressed to Pope Celestine I.

88. **The Church is apostolic in more than one sense:** See *Catechism of the Catholic Church*, nn. 857ff.

89. **"Preaching everywhere in country and town":** *To the Corinthians* 42:4–5. The concluding quotation is from the Septuagint Greek translation of Isaiah 60:17.

89. **Our Apostles knew through our Lord Jesus Christ":** *To the Corinthians* 44:1–2.

90. **St. Iranaeus wrote in 190 A.D. about the earlier popes:** *Adversus Haereses* 3.3.2.

CHAPTER 7

94. **Let's look more closely at what the Bible has to say about the saints in heaven:** See Patrick Madrid, *Any Friend of God's Is a Friend of Mine: A Biblical and Historical Explanation of the Catholic Doctrine of the Communion of Saints* (San Diego: Basilica Press, 1996).

96. **When He was present among them in the tabernacle:** See, for example, Exodus 13:21–22, 14:19–24, 19:9–16, 33:9–10; Leviticus 16:2,13; Numbers 9:15–22, 11:25, 12:5–10; Psalms 18:11–12; I Kings 8:10–11; 2 Chronicles 5:13–14; Daniel 7:13; Matthew 17:5.

101. **For me, she was a large obstacle on the way to Catholic faith:** See Scott Hahn, *Hail, Holy Queen: The Mother of God in the Word of God* (New York: Doubleday, 2001); "Biblical Theology and Marian Studies" in *Catholic for a Reason II: Scripture and the Mystery of the Mother of God*, 2d ed., Scott Hahn and Leon J. Suprenant Jr. (Steubenville, OH: Emmaus Road, 2004), pp. 199–227.

102. **The Greek grammatical form indicates that her "grace":** See Juniper Carol, O.F.M., *Fundamentals of Mariology* (New York: Benzinger Bros., 1957), p. 90.

103. **And since it is heavenly it is everlasting:** See Bernard J. Lefrois, S.V.D., *The Woman Clothed with the Sun: Individual or Collective* (Rome: Orbis Catholicus, 1954); Hans Urs von Balthasar and Joseph Cardinal Ratzinger, *Mary: The Church at the Source* (San Francisco: Ignatius Press, 2005), pp. 51–53.

104. **One was His mother, Mary:** See Pierre Barbet, *A Doctor at Calvary* (New York: Doubleday, 1979).

105. **That is how we approach her in intercessory prayer:** von Balthasar and Ratzinger, *Mary*, pp. 53–59.

107. **She remained "perpetually virgin":** See Geoffrey Graystone, S.M., *Virgin of All Virgins: The Interpretation of Luke 1:34* (Rome: Pontifical Biblical Commission, 1968); John J. Collins, S.J., "Our Lady's Vow of Virginity," in *Catholic Bible Quarterly* 5 (1943): 371–80.

108. **It was held firmly by the classic reformers:** For an excellent selection of the reformers' texts on the perpetual virginity, see Max Thurian, *Mary: Mother of All Christians* (New York: Herder and Herder, 1964), pp. 39–41. Thurian was writing as a Reformed pastor and theologian.

108. **Some modern Christian object (as did one ancient):** The fourth-
century heretic Helvidius misinterpreted a line from St. Matthew's
Gospel, which states that Joseph "knew her not until she had borne
a son" (Mt 1:25). He claimed that Matthew's use of "until" implies
that, after she had borne a son, Mary and Joseph pursued ordinary
marital relations. St. Jerome easily demolished Helvidius's
arguments, by noting other uses of "until" in the New Testament as
well as the Septuagint Greek Old Testament. Some of them yielded
quite odd results when read the way Helvidius was reading Matthew
1:25: "And Michal the daughter of Saul had no child until the day
of her death" (2 Sam 6:23). "And Samuel did not see Saul again
until the day of his death" (1 Sam 15:35). "He will not break a
bruised reed or quench a smoldering wick, till he brings justice to
victory" (Mt 12:20). None of these suggest a different state of
affairs after the term of the "until."

108. **From the first moment of her life, Mary was preserved from sin:**
See M. J. Scheeben, *Mariology: Volume II* (St. Louis: B. Herder Book
Co., 1947), pp. 57–139; Joseph Cardinal Ratzinger, *Daughter Zion:
Meditations on the Church's Marian Belief* (San Francisco: Ignatius Press,
1983), pp. 62–71; Fr. H. M. Manteau-Bonamy, O.P., *Immaculate
Conception and the Holy Spirit: The Marian Teachings of St. Maximilian Kolbe*
(Libertyville, IL: Marytown Press, 2001).

109. **"Now with the exception of the holy Virgin Mary":** *On Nature and
Grace* 36.42.

CHAPTER 8

112. **(In fact, I already have!):** See *The Lamb's Supper: The Mass as Heaven
on Earth* (New York: Doubleday, 1999); *Letter and Spirit: From Written
Text to Living Word in the Liturgy* (New York: Doubleday, 2005);
idem, "Worship in the Word: Toward a Liturgical Hermeneutic," in
Scott Hahn (ed.) *Letter & Spirit: Word, Worship, and the Mysteries*

(Steubenville, OH: St. Paul Center for Biblical Theology, 2005):
pp. 101–36.

112. **Reality contradicts the charge:** See Edward P. Sri, "A Walk Through
the Mass," in *Catholic for a Reason III: Scripture and the Mystery of the Mass*,
ed. Scott Hahn and Regis J. Flaherty (Steubenville, OH: Emmaus
Road Publishing, 2004), pp. 1–18.

112. **Catholics attending Mass on Sundays and holy days:** See
Normand Bonneau, *The Sunday Lectionary: Ritual Word, Paschal Shape*
(Collegeville, MN: Liturgical Press, 1998).

115. **Faithful to God's word, the Catholic Church continues:** See Jean
Daniélou, *The Bible and the Liturgy* (Notre Dame, IN: University of
Notre Dame Press, 1956).

118. **And so Catholics today endure even the jeers of other Christians:**
See James T. O'Connor, *Hidden Manna: A Theology of the Eucharist* (San
Francisco: Ignatius Press, 2005).

118. **The first Christians, like Catholics today:** See the comments of
A. G. Martimort in *The Church at Prayer* II (Collegeville, MN: Liturgi-
cal Press, 1992), pp. 247–48: and *Spirit*, p. 145: "What the pattern of
the tabernacle shown on the mountain (Ex 25:9) was for Moses, the
Letter to the Hebrews and the Apocalypse are for the Church." Again:
"The spirit of the Letter to the Hebrews and the Apocalypse enlivens
the early Eucharistic Prayers of all the Christian rites and permeates
their ceremonial." Also see Hahn, *Letter and Spirit*, pp. 144–46;
M. M. Schaefer, "Heavenly and Earthly Liturgies: Patristic
Prototypes, Medieval Perspectives, and a Contemporary Application,
Worship 70 (1996), pp. 482–505; Michael Barber, "The Mass and the
Apocalypse," in *Catholic For a Reason III: Scripture and the Mystery of the
Mass*, pp. 109–21; Leonard L. Thompson, *The Book of Revelation:
Apocalypse and Empire* (New York: Oxford University Press, 1990);
David Aune, *The Cultic Setting of Realized Eschatology in Early Christianity*
(Leiden, Netherlands: Brill, 1972); John Koenig, *The Feast of the World's*

Redemption: Eucharistic Origins and Christian Mission (Harrisburg, PA: Trinity Press International, 2000), pp. 167–68; Gregory Dix, *The Shape of the Liturgy* (London: Dacre Press, 1945), p. 28. See the following *Catechism* paragraphs: 1090, 1111, 1136–39 1187, 1244, 1326, 1329, 1402–1405, 1419, 1589, 2642, 2770–71, 2776, 2816, 2837.

118. **This is the ancient and perennial Catholic understanding of the Mass:** See Mike Aquilina, *The Mass of the Early Christians* (Huntington, IN: Our Sunday Visitor, 2001).

119. **The first Christians were "the assembly of the firstborn":** See Joseph Ratzinger, *A New Song for the Lord* (New York: Crossroad, 1997), p. 129; Joseph Cardinal Ratzinger, *The Spirit of the Liturgy* (San Francisco: Ignatius Press, 2000), pp. 185–86.

119. **The blood of Christ—the cup of His blood—purifies sinners:** See Maurice de la Taille, S.J., *The Mystery of Faith, Book I: The Sacrifice of Our Lord* (New York: Sheed & Ward, 1940); Thomas J. Nash, "He Died Once, But His Sacrifice Lives On: The Mass as Sacrifice," in *Catholic for a Reason III: Scripture and the Mystery of the Mass*, pp. 49–63.

121. **"and on the Lord's own day gather yourselves together":** *Didache* 14.1; see also 14.2–3.

121. **St. Ignatius of Antioch, writing only a few years after the death of the Apostles:** *Ephesians* 5.2; *Trallians* 7.2; *Philadelphians* 4.

121. **"Take heed, then, to have but one Eucharist":** *Philadelphians* 4.

121. **Ignatius defined heretics:** *Smyrnaeans* 6.2.

121. **In another of his letters, he even compares himself:** *Romans* 1.

121. **A priest is, by definition, someone who offers sacrifice:** See Louis A. Ruprecht, *Was Greek Thought Religious: On the Use and Abuse of Hellenism, from Rome to Romanticism* (New York: Palgrave, 2002); Fustel de Coulanges, *The Ancient City: A Classic Study of the Religious and Civil Institutions of Ancient Greece and Rome* (Garden City, NY: Doubleday Anchor Books, 1956).

122. **"Let that eucharist alone be considered valid":** *Smyrnaeans* 8.1.

124. **That saving fire is what Catholics call purgatory:** For a helpful explanation to this doctrine, see Michael J. Taylor, *Purgatory* (Huntington, IN: Our Sunday Visitor, 1998); Curtis A. Martin, "The Burning Truth about Purgatory," in *Catholic for a Reason: Scripture and the Mystery of the Family of God,* ed. Scott Hahn and Leon J. Suprenant Jr. (Steubenville, OH: Emmaus Road Publishing, 1998), pp. 291–310.

CHAPTER 9

128. **In this chapter, I'll respond to some of the common objections against Catholic doctrine on the papacy:** Also very helpful are the following books: Scott Butler, Norman Dahlgren, and David Hess, *Jesus, Peter, and the Keys: A Scriptural Handbook on the Papacy* (Santa Barbara, CA: Queenship Publishing, 1997); Stephen K. Ray, *Upon This Rock: St. Peter and the Primacy of Rome in Scripture and the Early Church* (San Francisco: Ignatius Press, 1999); Vladimir Soloviev, *The Russian Church and the Papacy* (San Diego: Catholic Answers, 2002).

128. **They're misunderstandings in most cases:** For questions not treated here, see Patrick Madrid, *Pope Fiction: Answers to 30 Myths and Misconceptions about the Papacy* (Rancho Santa Fe, CA: Basilica Press, 2000).

135. **"They have not the heritage of Peter":** *On Penitence* 1.7.

135. **"He who deserts the chair of Peter":** *On the Unity of the Church* 4.

135. **"I speak with the successor of the fisherman":** Letter 15.

CHAPTER 10

139. **While the ordering principle behind *systematic theology* is the logical progression of doctrines:** See Scott Hahn, *Letter & Spirit,* pp. 16–19. See also my chapter entitled " 'Search the Scriptures': Reading the Old Testament with Jesus, John, and Thomas

Aquinas," in *Scripture Matters: Essays on Reading the Bible from the Heart of the Church* (Steubenville, OH: Emmaus Road Publishing, 2003), pp. 49–63.

CHAPTER II

144. **Adam is intentionally portrayed as a royal firstborn:** See my *A Father Who Keeps His Promises: God's Covenant Love in Scripture* (Cincinnati: Servant Books, 1998), pp. 37–55.

145. **This view is borne out not only in the teaching of the Catholic Church:** See Pope John Paul II, *Dies Domini*, Apostolic Letter on Keeping the Lord's Day Holy (July 5, 1998), n. 8; see also *Catechism of the Catholic Church*, n. 288.

145. **... but also in the writings of the ancient rabbis:** See, for example, *Sifre Deuteronomy;* the *Book of Jubilees* (36.7), and *1 Enoch* (69:15–27).

145. **Moderns scholars have referred to God's seventh-day blessing as the "Cosmic Covenant":** See, for example, Robert Murray, *The Cosmic Covenant* (London: Sheed & Ward, 1992).

146. **This, the Original Sin, is a disaster of cosmic proportions:** For my thoughts on the fall, see *First Comes Love: Finding Your Family in the Church and the Trinity* (New York: Doubleday, 2002), pp. 62–79; *A Father Who Keeps*, pp. 57–76. One of the best (if not *the* best) articulations of the theology surrounding creation and Original Sin is found in Scheeben's *The Mysteries of Christianity*, pp. 201–310.

146. **Yet the ancient Christians, and their modern descendants, could sing of the fall from grace:** See the *Exultet*, the opening song of the Easter Vigil liturgy.

148. **As Adam had been made in God's image and likeness:** See John A. Davies, *A Royal Priesthood: Literary and Intertextual Perspectives on an Image of Israel in Exodus 19.6* (New York: T & T Clark, 2004).

148. **And just as the original fall had resulted in exile:** Scott W. Hahn,

"Canon, Cult and Covenant," in C. Bartholomew, S. W. Hahn (eds.), *Canon and Biblical Interpretation* (Grand Rapids: Zondervan, 2006), pp. 214–17.

CHAPTER 12

151. **He establishes the only lasting royal house in the Old Testament:** On the Davidic Kingdom covenant traditions in the Old and New Testament, see Y. S. Chae, *Jesus as the Eschatological Davidic Shepherd: Studies in the Old Testament, Second Temple Judaism, and in the Gospel of Matthew* (Tubingen: Mohr Siebeck, 2006); Antti Laato, *A Star Is Rising: The Historical Development of the Old Testament Royal Ideology and the Rise of the Jewish Messianic Expectation* (Atlanta: Scholars Press, 1997); C. Meyers, "The Israelite Empire: In Defense of King Solomon," in P. O'Connor and D. N. Freedman (eds.), *Backgrounds for the Bible* (Winona Lake, IN: Eisenbrauns, 1987), pp. 181–97; Brian M. Nolan, *The Royal Son of God* (Gottingen: Vanderhoeck & Ruprecht, 1979); Tomoo Ishida, *The Royal Dynasties in Ancient Israel: A Study on the Formation and Development of Royal-Dynastic Ideology* (New York: Walter de Gruyter, 1977); A. G. Hebert, *The Throne of David: A Study of the Fulfillment of the Old Testament in Jesus Christ and His Church* (London: Faber & Faber, 1956).

156. *The Davidic monarch was the Son of God:* John J. Collins, *The Scepter and the Star: The Messiahs of the Dead Sea Scrolls and Other Ancient Literature* (New York: Doubleday, 1995), p. 163; "The individual most often designated as 'the son of God' in the Hebrew Bible is undoubtedly the Davidic king, or his eschatological counterpart." Also see Joseph A. Fitzmyer, *The One Who Is to Come* (Grand Rapids: Eerdmans, 2007), pp. 33–55.

157. *The House of David was inextricably bound to Jerusalem, particularly Mt. Zion:* See Theodore Mascarenhas, *The Missionary Function of Israel* (New

York: University Press of America, 2005); Norbert Lohfink and Erich Zenger, *The God of Israel and the Nations: Studies in Isaiah and the Psalms* (Collegeville, MN: Liturgical Press, 2000).

157. **The Davidic Kingdom at *Zion* thus marks the first time Israel was called to welcome gentiles:** The Mosaic covenant at *Sinai* had been strictly national and exclusive, whereas the Davidic covenant at *Zion* was international and all-inclusive. The Psalms celebrate—and justify from a theological perspective—this state of affairs, just as the Prophets envision its restoration. Just as the Mosaic covenant is embodied in the Pentateuch, so the literary corpus of the Davidic covenant may be found in Wisdom literature (e.g., Proverbs, Job, Ecclesiastes). These are the biblical books with the most universal reach, appealing not to the Mosaic laws of Israel's polity, but to creation, the natural law, and family values and relations, all of which convey a universal message for all peoples. See K. I. Parker, *Wisdom and Law in the Reign of Solomon* (Lewiston, NY: Mellen Biblical Press, 1992).

158. ***The Queen Mother* became an important part of the royal government:** See Edward Sri, *Queen Mother: A Biblical Theology of Mary's Queenship* (Steubenville, OH: Emmaus Road Publishing, 2005); George Montague, *Our Father, Our Mother: Mary and the Faces of God* (Steubenville, OH: Franciscan University Press, 1990), pp. 89–101; Niels-Erik A. Andreasen, "The Role of the Queen Mother in Israelite Society," *Catholic Biblical Quarterly* 45 (1982): 174–94; Carol Smith, "Queenship in Israel: The Cases of Bathsheba, Jezebel and Athaliah," in John Day (ed.), *King and Messiah in Israel and the Ancient Near East* (Sheffield: Sheffield Academic Press, 1998), pp. 142–62; K. Spanier, "The Queen Mother in the Judean Royal Court," in Athalya Brenner, ed., *A Feminist Companion to Samuel and Kings* (Sheffield: Sheffield Academic Press, 1994), pp. 186–95; Susan Ackerman, "The Queen Mother and the Cult of Ancient Israel,"

Journal of Biblical Literature 112 (1993): 385–401; Zafria Ben-Barak, "The Status and Right of the Gebira," *Journal of Biblical Literature* 110 (1991): 23–34.

158–159. **The king had many servants (in I Kgs 4:7 there are twelve):** See T. N. D. Mettinger, *Solomonic State Officials: A Study of the Civil Officials of the Israelite Monarchy* (Lund: Gleerup, 1971).

159. **The word for "thank offering" is *todah* in Hebrew:** The exact quote ("In the coming [messianic] age, all sacrifices will cease except the *todah* sacrifice. This will never cease in all eternity") is taken from the *Pesiqta* I; cited by Hartmut Gese, *Essays in Biblical Theology* (Minneapolis: Augsburg, 1981), p. 133. See Jean LaPorte, *Eucharistia in Philo* (New York: Edwin Mellen, 1983), 31–34.

162. **That is to say, the fallen tent of David is he who shall arise:** *Pss. Sol.* 17:4; 4QFlorilegium (4Q 174) I I, 7–13; cf. 4Q252 V, 1–5; cf. Sir 45:25; 47:11; 4Q504 (4QDibHam^a) I–2 IV, 6–8; *T. Jud.*22:3. See William Horbury, *Jewish Messianism and the Cult of Christ* (London: SCM Press, 1998), pp. 36–63; idem, *Messianism among Jews and Christians* (New York: T&T Clark, 2003), pp. 35–64.

CHAPTER 13

166. **And He had the royal pedigree to prove it:** Matthew's genealogy begins with Abraham, but it centers on the kingdom of David. The four fixed points are the life of Abraham, the reign of David, the fall of the house of David at the Babylonian exile, and the arrival of Jesus. Matthew compresses the generations so that they fall into three groups of fourteen—the numeral that, in Hebrew, is spelled out by David's name *(DVD)*. In Hebrew, as in Latin, letters stand for numbers; so Jesus' Davidic genealogy repeatedly reinforces his identity with the royal family line.

169. **For most of the gospel he is traveling there (9:51–19:27):** For a broader treatment of the ecclesiological significance of the Temple,

see G. K. Beale, *The Temple and the Church's Mission: A Biblical Theology of the Dwelling Place of God* (Downers Grove, IL: InterVarsity Press, 2004); also see Stephen T. Um, *The Theme of Temple Christology in John's Gospel* (New York: T & T Clark, 2006); Alan R. Kerr, *The Temple of Jesus' Body: The Temple Theme in the Gospel of John* (New York: T & T Clark, 2002).

170. **The king bestows authority symbolically with "the keys"**: See the comments of recent Protestant biblical scholars on Mt 16 and Is 22: W. F. Albright and C. S. Mann, *Matthew* (New York: Doubleday, 1971), pp. 196–97: "Is. 22:15ff undoubtedly lies behind this saying. The keys are the symbol of authority . . . the same authority as that vested in the vizier, the master of the . . . royal household in ancient Israel. Eliakim is described as having the same authority in Is. 22 . . . It is of considerable importance that in other contexts, when the disciplinary affairs of the community are being discussed (Mt 18:18), the symbol of the keys is absent, since the sayings apply in those instances to a wider circle." Also see Bruce Chilton, "Shebna, Eliakim, and the Promise to Peter," in J. Neusner et al. (eds.), *The Social World of Formative Judaism* (Philadelphia: Fortress, 1988), p. 322; Tord Fornberg, "Peter: The High Priest of the New Covenant," *Southeast Asia Journal of Theology* 4 (1986), p. 113: Peter is presented as some kind of successor to the high priest. . . . Peter stands out as a kind of Chief Rabbi who binds and looses in the sense of declaring something to be forbidden or permitted." See the encyclical of Pope Leo XIII, *Satis Cognitum* ("On the Unity of the Church"; June 29, 1896): "The Church is typified not only as an *edifice* but as a *kingdom* and everyone knows that the keys constitute the usual sign of governing authority. Wherefore when Christ promised to give to Peter the keys of the kingdom of heaven, He promised to give him power and authority over the Church" (*Papal Teachings: The Church* [Boston: St. Paul, 1961], p. 322).

171. **Indeed, whenever we find Jesus breaking bread:** On the
significance of the *todah* in the New Testament, see Joseph
Ratzinger, *Feast of Faith* (San Francisco: Ignatius Press, 1986), pp.
51–60; James Swetnam, *"Zebach Toda* in Tradition: A Study of
'Sacrifice of Praise'," *Filologia Neotestamentaria* 15 (2002): 65–86;
idem, "A Liturgical Approach to Hebrews 13," in Scott Hahn (ed.),
Letter & Spirit: The Word of God and the People of God (Steubenville, OH:
St. Paul Center for Biblical Theology, 2006), pp. 159–73; Tim
Gray, "From Jewish Passover to Christian Eucharist: The Todah
Sacrifice as Backdrop for the Last Supper," in *Catholic for a Reason III:
Scripture and the Mystery of the Mass,* 67–76.

CHAPTER 14

173. **Since Luke's Gospel provides the greatest abundance of
kingdom-related details:** For a more thorough treatment of these
themes, see Michael E. Fuller, *The Restoration of Israel: Israel's Regathering
and the Fate of the Nations* (Berlin: Walter de Gruyter, 2006); Scott
Hahn, "Kingdom and Church in Luke-Acts: From Davidic
Christology to Kingdom Ecclesiology," in Craig Bartholomew, Joel
Green, Anthony Thiselton (eds.); *Reading Luke: Interpretation, Reflections,
Formation* (Grand Rapids, MI: Zondervan, 2005), pp. 294–326.

182. **The Davidic kingdom finds historic fulfillment in the Catholic
Church:** This thesis concerning the identity of the Davidic
kingdom and the Church can be confirmed by other passages in
Acts, but it will suffice to focus on James's concluding statements at
the Jerusalem council (Acts 15). James cements the council's
decision to embrace gentile converts by quoting Amos 9:11–12:
"After this I will return, and I will rebuild the dwelling skenè of
David . . . that the rest of men may seek the Lord, and all the
Gentiles who are called by my name" (Acts 15:13–18). The
"dwelling" or "tent" of David referred to by Amos (Amos 9:11) is

the Davidic kingdom, which at its peak incorporated Edom (cf. Amos 9:12a) and other gentile nations (Ammon, Moab, Aram, etc.) which may be "the nations who are called by my name" (Amos 9:12b). In other words, James observes that the Davidic kingdom was an empire incorporating gentile peoples, and Amos prophesied that this arrangement would be restored in the last days. He sees the fulfillment of Amos's prophecy—i.e., the restoration of the Davidic empire—in the incorporation of gentiles into the Church as related by "Simeon" before the whole council. See David W. Pao, *Acts and the Isaianic New Exodus* (Tubingen: Mohr Siebeck 2000), p. 138: "The promise to rebuild and restore the Davidic kingdom is explicitly made at the point in the narrative of Acts that focuses on defining the people of God. The Amos quotation of Acts 15 shows that . . . the development of the early Christian community is also understood within the paradigm of the anticipation of the Davidic kingdom. The *christological* focus of the David tradition should be supplemented by an *ecclesiological* one."

183. **"The story of David brings out all the strengths and weaknesses of the beginnings of the religious institution of the kingdom":** Raymond Brown, S.S., "Communicating the Divine and Human in Scripture," *Origins* 22.1 (May 14, 1992): 5–6, emphasis mine.

184. **It would be a field sown with both wheat and weeds:** See J. P. Arendzen, *Men and Manners in the Days of Christ* (St. Louis: Herder, 1928), pp. 34–35: "What, then, are the texts which have persuaded some people of Christ's mistaken expectation in this matter? 'Amen, I say unto you, there are some of them that here stand by, who shall in no-wise taste death, till they see the Kingdom of God come with power (Mark ix, 1) . . . Here, so it is said, it is plain that Christ looks forward to His coming within the lifetime of at least some of those then living. We answer that the whole question depends on what is meant by this coming of the kingdom in power and the coming of

the Son of Man in His kingdom. The word kingdom occurs some
sixty times in the Gospel of St. Matthew, as many in St. Luke, and
thirty times in St. Mark; it cannot be so difficult to ascertain its
meaning. It usually means, not a kingdom away from this earth, a
kingdom in the skies, a kingdom at the end of time, God's final
kingdom after the day of judgment, the kingdom where Christ in His
unveiled glory shall reign amongst the angels and saints, but the
kingdom of truth and grace, which He came to found on earth,
the Catholic Church. There are scores of parables to show this. The
kingdom is like unto ten virgins, five of whom were foolish and five
wise, but in heaven above there are no fools, only on this earth. The
kingdom is like unto a field in which the wheat and tares are sown,
but Christ Himself explains: 'the field is this world.' The kingdom is
like unto a net cast into the sea, catching good fishes and bad, but
such a catch is only possible here upon earth . . . Thus we might go
through all the parables, showing that Christ's kingdom is a human,
though divine, kingdom on this earth in which Christ reigns, long
before He comes again upon the clouds of heaven. To Peter He gave
the keys of the kingdom of heaven, that what Peter loosed on earth
might be loosed also in heaven . . . It is is clear that 'the coming of the
Son of Man in His kingdom with power' means the evident and
triumphant establishment of the Catholic Church of Christ . . ."

184. **"The Church is already now the kingdom of Christ"**: *Meditations on the Psalms* 92.4.

184. **"The kingdom is already on earth, and the Church is already in heaven"**: Quoted in Cardinal Christoph Schonborn, *From Death to Life* (San Francisco: Ignatius Press, 1995), p. 83.; reprinted in S. Hahn (ed.), *Letter and Spirit II: The Authority of Mystery* (Steubenville, OH: St. Paul Center, 2006), pp. 217–34.

185. **"when He appears we shall be like Him"**: Charles Cardinal

Journet, *The Theology of the Church* (San Francisco: Ignatius Press, 2004), p. 377: "As revelation presents her to us, the Church is a *Kingdom*, the Kingdom in which God in Christ triumphs over the wickedness of the world, in which God can reign over men already here below through the Cross of Christ and, later on, by the glory of Christ. The Kingdom, indeed, like its King, has two phases: one veiled and on pilgrimage, the other glorious and definitive."

186. **"you have come to *Mount Zion* and to the city of the living God"**: See K. Son, *Zion Symbolism in Hebrews: Hebrew 12:18–24 as a Hermeneutical Key to the Epistle* (Waynesboro, GA: Paternoster Biblical Monographs, 2005). Various early patristic figures (e.g., Epiphanius, Eusebius) identify Zion as the mountain on which the Cenacle or Upper Room was located, and where the "mother church" was located, which survived Titus's siege of Jerusalem in 70 A.D. The Upper Room on Zion thus evoked a very profound (threefold) theological symbolism—as the place: (1) where Christ ratified the New Covenant, by instituting the Eucharist (LK 22); (2) where the resurrected Christ first appeared to the Apostles, and instituted the sacrament of confession (Jn 20:19–23); (3) where the Holy Spirit fell upon Mary and the Apostles at Pentecost, which marked the "birth" of the Church of the New Covenant (Ac 2).

187. **And His kingdom is the Church:** See *The Dogmatic Constitution on the Church* (Lumen Gentium): "To carry out the will of the Father, Christ inaugurated the kingdom of heaven on earth and revealed to us his mystery; by his obedience he brought about our redemption. The Church—that is, the kingdom of Christ already present in mystery—grows visibly through the power of God in the world" (no. 3). See "Select Themes of Ecclesiology" (1984): "To limit the Church to her purely earthly and visible dimension is unthinkable . . . The origins of the Church and the advent of the Kingdom of God

are presented here in perfect synchronicity... The Church is not a mere sign (*sacramentum tantum*) but a sign in which the reality signified is present (*res et sacramentum*) as the reality of the Kingdom" (*International Theological Commission: Texts and Documents, 1965–1985* [San Francisco: Ignatius Press, 1989], pp. 301–4. See the encyclical of Pope Pius IX, *Vix dum a Nobis:* "In fact, the Creator and Redeemer of the human race has certainly founded the Church as his visible Kingdom on earth." And Pope St. Pius X: "The Church is a kingdom whose master is none other than God; her mission is so great that it goes beyond frontiers and makes of the peoples of every language and every nation, one family" (*Papal Teachings: The Church* [Boston: St. Paul, 1962], pp. 240, 397). See *The Catechism of the Catholic Church* (nos. 541, 670–71, 768–69, 865). See F. X. Durrwell, *The Resurrection: A Biblical Study* (New York: Sheed & Ward, 1960), p. 270: "So [the Church] exists fully in two different periods of time... she dwells in heaven but also journeys on earth. She does not exist somewhere between the two times, but actually in both simultaneously... Thus the Church bears the marks of two opposite states. She leads a mysterious, heavenly existence, and she is also a visible empirical reality.... In her mysterious reality the church is indeed the Kingdom of God... but as perceived by the senses, she is only its sign and instrument." See Avery Dulles, "The Church and the Kingdom," in Eugene LaVerdiere (ed.), *A Church for All Peoples* (Collegeville, MN: Liturgical Press, 1993), pp. 17–18: "If one looks on both the kingdom and the Church as existing proleptically within history and definitively at the close of history, it becomes more difficult to see how they differ." In sharp contrast, Richard McBrien considers the identification of Church and kingdom as "the most serious pre-Vatican II ecclesiological misunderstanding" (*Catholicism* [London: Geoffrey Chapman, 1981], p. 686).

CHAPTER 15

190. "a transference from the state in which man is born a son of the first Adam": Council of Trent, session 6.4.

190. "the notion of justification would have escaped the shallow and muddled treatment that has so often disfigured it": *The Mysteries of Christianity*, p. 623.